Practical Methods of Moral Education

Language and Christian Belief (Macmillan 1958)
Language and the Pursuit of Truth (C.U.P. 1960)
Reason and Morals (C.U.P. 1961)
Public Schools and Private Practice (Allen & Unwin 1962)
Philosophy and Religion (O.U.P. 1965)
Logic and Sexual Morality (Penguin 1965)
Thinking with Concepts (C.U.P. 1966)
Equality (Hutchinson 1966)
Education and the Concept of Mental Health (Routledge 1968)
Introduction to Moral Education (Penguin 1968)
Philosophy (Heinemann 1969)
Moral Thinking (Heinemann 1970)
Education in Religion and the Emotions (Heinemann 1971)

JOHN WILSON

Director of Research, Farmington Trust Research Unit, Oxford

Practical Methods of
Moral Education

HEINEMANN EDUCATIONAL
BOOKS · LONDON

Heinemann Educational Books Ltd
LONDON · EDINBURGH · MELBOURNE
SINGAPORE · JOHANNESBURG · IBADAN
HONG KONG · TORONTO · AUCKLAND
NAIROBI · KUALA LUMPUR · NEW DELHI

ISBN 0 435 80927 X
© John Wilson 1972
First published 1972

Published by Heinemann Educational Books Ltd
48 Charles Street, London W1X 8AH

Printed in Great Britain by
C. Tinling & Co Ltd, London and Prescot

Contents

Contents

Preface

The research worker in education has a hard time of it. On the one hand, there are numerous demands made on him to produce, if not 'the answer', at least definite and practical recommendations which teachers and other educators can put into effect. He will feel the force of this, but will say to himself 'That's all very well, but there is not much point in making practical recommendations unless I can prove their worth: and it takes a great deal of time and money to do this. The history of education is littered with examples of "new methods", recommended more by educational fashion or political prejudice than by argument or scientific proof, which survive by inertia or die off when the fashion or the prejudice changes: and to add to these would merely make confusion worse confounded'. On the other hand, there is the demand for conceptual and scientific rigour: and here he may feel '*That's* all very well, but meanwhile there is a desperate practical need: on this basis it looks as if the first generation to benefit by our results will be great-grandchildren, by which time conditions will have changed radically, even if we have not yet blown up the world'.

This is not the total *impasse* that it seems: but we must be careful to escape from it in the right direction. One common escape is simply to compromise. We may find ourselves saying 'O.K., well, we'll just have to cut our coat to fit our cloth. We will do something that might plausibly be called "research"; but we will lower our academic standards, and not worry too much about assessment or proof. We shall call it "action research" or "operational research" or "research-and-development", and we shall have very general aims – encouraging teachers to try new methods, getting a feed-back from them, and seeing if the methods are (in some rather nebulous sense) "successful". We shall have only short-term research projects, so as to make sure that they are "practical" and "operational": and we shall rely heavily on trial-and-error, teachers' verdicts, and public opinion in the educational world.'

Of course this is not completely silly. First, trial-and-error and (in a loose sense of the word) experiment 'in the field' are very useful for any kind of research. Secondly, there are plenty of 'practical' research projects of which we might want to say, vaguely but importantly, 'they seem to be doing some good', or 'they seem to be getting somewhere', and which should therefore be encouraged. Thirdly, there are a number of desirable objectives which need to be reached, though they are in no sense research objectives: e.g. arousing public concern, stimulating teachers, providing materials, and so forth. As long as these quite different aims and criteria are kept clear, projects that operate on this basis may be very useful. But the danger is obvious: in so far as the results of such projects actually influence or change school practice, we have to have some assurance that they are changing it in a desirable direction. This means that, even if we do not always have to have some scientifically rigorous method of assessment, we must at least be absolutely clear about the specific *aims* of whatever it is we are selling and about how, logically, what we are selling seems *prima facie* to fit such aims. For without such clarity we shall sell nothing coherent: we shall simply be promoting some current fashion, perhaps today a fashion for 'integration', 'open-ended discussion', 'child-centred teaching', or some other more or less incomprehensibly-titled set of practices.

Another way out of the *impasse* seems to be more profitable, and I hope justifies this book. It is to use an already-established set of aims, clearly stated and broken down into as much detail as possible, on which to base a consideration of certain methods which are in effect logically required by these aims. The crucial part of this involves *explaining* to teachers and other educators, with the utmost care and clarity, just *how* these methods are required by the aims. What is needed, in other words, is not a somewhat hit-and-miss set of recommendations of detailed methods, techniques and materials, which subsequent research may show to be totally useless or positively harmful: but rather something which contributes to greater understanding of the *nature*, *logic* and *point* of certain general methods or approaches which, in some form or other, must be used. Thus I shall claim that the concept of a morally educated person necessarily involves certain abilities or attainments connected with the use of language: and I devote Part II of this book to explaining the sense in which this is true, what is meant here by 'the use of language', and what methods of approach might in principle succeed in giving pupils these abilities and attainments;

ending up with a detailed description of how one particular context
of language-using ('discussion') may be defined and taught.

Whatever the merits of this particular book, I feel reasonably
confident that this is the kind of book that practical educators need.
There is already a wealth of material – textbooks, visual aids,
suggestions for particular techniques, etc. – from which the teacher
may select: the difficulty which he ought to feel is how to select
and what he is really trying to do. This is a difficulty which will not
be solved by the production of more materials – nor even entirely
solved by stringent academic research. The teacher must somehow
get clear in his own mind about the point and logic of possible
methods, about the *criteria* of selection. It is not easy: but it is
essential. Certainly there is no point in adding to the vast and
growing morass of literature about education: my intention here
is, by draining a little of the swamp, to give practical educators a
bit of firm ground to stand on.

J. B. W.

Farmington Trust Research Unit, Oxford, 1972

Introduction

Progress in moral education[1] may be hindered by factors over which the educator has little or no control – shortage of time and money, the crippling background of many pupils' lives, and so on: but it may also be hindered by unnecessary obstacles in the minds of the educators themselves.

These are twofold. First, people may be muddled about what they should *try* to achieve under this heading: about the aims of moral education, or what it means to be 'morally educated'. We have clarified these aims at length elsewhere,[2] and they reappear in Part I of this book in a form suitable for practical use. I shall not weary the reader by a further defence of them here. There is, of course, always room for philosophical dispute; but I would hope that most readers are sufficiently in agreement to devote their full attention to the methods. At this stage of the subject the most urgent need is that these methods, and others like them, should be understood and tried.

Secondly, however, many people are dominated, consciously or unconsciously, by a *simpliste* model of how moral education gets done. For them, it is *all* a matter of 'personal example', 'pupil-teacher relationships', 'the atmosphere of the school', 'early socialization', 'reading the great writers of the past', 'having a faith to live by', 'coming face to face with nature', or whatever method the person wants to put his money on. What we may call the 'infection' model of morality, whereby 'goodness' somehow infects or inspires the pupil, radiating and infiltrating from 'good' teachers, parents, heroes, works of art or natural surroundings, is only one example of such *simpliste* models. Others are associated with 'faith', 'social adjustment', 'creativity', certain psychodynamic techniques, and so forth.

[1] The reader may prefer other titles: 'learning to live', 'personal relationships', 'social education', 'health education', or whatever. This doesn't matter much.

[2] *Introduction to Moral Education* (Wilson, Williams and Sugarman: Penguin, 1968); *Education in Religion and the Emotions* (Wilson: Heinemann, 1971). Hereafter I shall refer to these as *I.M.E.* and *E.R.E.* respectively.

Of course there is *something* to be said for all these. But – as we shall see more clearly later on[1] – no single, overall model of this kind is possible. A clear and detailed grasp of the aims of moral education makes it obvious that *many different* abilities and attainments are required, which necessarily involve many different methods. Only somebody who had a very simple-minded picture of the 'good' or the 'moral' person possessing some *one* attribute – as if being 'good' was like being tall or being red-blooded – would make this mistake. But the temptations to make it are very strong (even when it has been pointed out): and I want to stress here that no progress is likely to be made in methods of moral education unless educators are prepared to keep a genuinely open mind.

In two earlier publications of this Research Unit[2] we tried to outline the logic and the aims of moral education: and we also made some very brief and tentative suggestions about possible methods of achieving those aims.[3] Here I am concerned with expanding and clarifying four of these methods or approaches, which will be dealt with here under the titles of 'Moral Thinking' (I), 'Language and Communication' (II), 'Rules and Contracts' (III), and 'The School Community' (IV). Naturally the reader must not suppose that I can deal at all fully with any of these areas, each of which is in itself an enormous field for sociological and psychological research. What I shall do is to consider them very briefly, and offer some practical suggestions for teaching in each of them.

The point of the book as a whole is explained in the Preface. My reasons for choosing these particular methods are as follows:

1. They are *practical:* that is, teachers and educators in schools and elsewhere can start using them at once. Other methods might require some lengthy retraining of teachers, or major changes in the examination system, or a drastic reorganization of the whole educational setup. These matters are partly in the hands of local educational authorities, or of the D.E.S., or of other organizations outside the control of the practising teacher. They are important, but I am not concerned with them here.

2. They are in principle relevant to all types of educational institutions. Obviously their precise application, and the specific contexts and teaching-techniques required, will vary with the age of the pupils (and of course with other factors as well): but the

[1] p. 93 ff.
[2] *I.M.E.* and *E.R.E.*
[3] *I.M.E.*, pp. 409-13.

methods themselves can be applied right through from the primary school up to and including adult education. Educators are perhaps most accustomed to this general area of thinking chiefly in the context of the secondary school: but its relevance to universities and colleges of education, technology, liberal arts and so forth should be plain enough.

3. We have reason to believe that these particular methods are amongst those likely to be effective. It would take too long to spell out the evidence for this: some of it is a matter of what is logically required for the notion of a morally educated person, some derives from specific research findings, and some has the form of *a priori* probabilities of the kind mentioned in our first publication. At the same time, it must be understood that no fully objective and detailed assessment of these methods has been undertaken. Such assessment depends on the availability of reliable tests and assessment-methods, which we and others are working on at the present time. I have said something elsewhere[1] about how the teacher may try to assess their merits for himself in the meantime.

4. Last but not least, these methods are not everywhere in common use. I am aware, of course, that some of them are far from unknown to those who teach the lower age-ranges of children, remedial classes, 'backward', 'maladjusted' or 'non-communicating' children, etc.; and, in some degree, to teachers in secondary schools, sixth-form colleges, and higher education. But (with respect) I do not think that most of the work actually done, useful though it may be, is backed by a coherent rationale or organized into an effective pattern. Hence my hope is that even those (comparatively few) teachers who have long been working in this general area will find this book useful; and I should add to this the claim that these methods need, in any case, to be very much more widely (as well as more coherently) used.

Of course there are many other methods and approaches which are easier to think of, and perhaps no less valuable: and I do not want to convey the impression that they are to be disdained. For instance, a common approach is to discuss a particular *topic* with children, and try to educate them morally with respect to that topic: 'sex', 'war', 'race prejudice', 'old people', and 'the family' are typical examples. But it is less easy, though probably

[1] *Moral Education and the Curriculum* (Pergamon Press, 1969): also *The Assessment of Morality* (forthcoming).

more important, to think about how we can help pupils to discuss rationally at all: how we can give them the habit of using thought and language to solve problems (as we shall try to do in Part II). Here again my impression is that much of our educational practice in this field is disorganized and not based on a clear understanding of the relevant objectives: there is a tendency to keep the progressive pot boiling, no doubt in interesting and stimulating ways, but without any very coherent ideas about what exactly we are trying to cook.

When I say that these methods are practical and effective, I do not of course mean either that they are easy or that they work like magic charms. Teachers hardly need to be told that the merits of any educational method depend largely on the enthusiasm and imagination of the person using it; and, since these methods are not as yet widely adopted, it may require some degree of initiative to use them at all. But all of them need to be fully understood for what they are before being used. A good deal of such understanding involves grasping the aims, or one might almost say the *logic*, of the methods: and I hope that practising teachers who want to go ahead and use them will bear with me while, in what follows, I try to explain this logic at some length. Even after a fairly clear grasp of it has been achieved, there will be of course plenty of room for experiment and change in the details of the methods. Indeed it may well turn out that I have been wrong to stress certain practical features at the expense of others, or misguided in suggesting the efficacy of this as opposed to that arrangement. This does not very much matter: it simply emphasises the point that, given some kind of lead in this direction, teachers themselves are by far the best people to work out the details of such methods with their own particular children, whom they alone can really know, and in their own schools and conditions of work, with which they alone are fully familiar.

PART I

Moral Thinking[1]

I begin with a method which is, in essence, perhaps the simplest of the four to understand: but which is also controversial. It is the method of acquainting the pupils, consciously and overtly, with morality as a subject or area of thought: making them aware of the skills, techniques and qualities required to get the right answers to moral questions (the 'methodology' of the subject) and giving them practice in solving moral problems.

Some may still have doubts about what this 'methodology' should be. I have argued elsewhere[2] that it is possible to establish a set of qualities, or 'moral components', which are logically required by anybody who seriously sets out to answer questions of the form 'What ought I to do?' and to act on the answers. These components are not the peculiar property of any particular faith, creed, set of moral values or partisan beliefs, but qualities and rules of procedure which define what it is to be 'reasonable' or 'serious' about morality. I have also argued[3] that, as well as the danger of the partisan teaching (or indoctrination) of a particular morality, there is also the danger of excessive vagueness: talk about 'sensitivity', 'maturity', 'caring', etc. is not necessarily partisan, but is unhelpfully global. For these reasons it is important to list the components with clarity and care, and in detail.

Putting these components or qualities before pupils may be called a 'direct' method of moral education, because we are here directly and openly *telling* pupils what it means for a person to be morally

---

[1] For pupil-teacher material relevant to this Part of the book, see bibliography.

[2] *I.M.E.*, Introduction and Chapter 4.

[3] *E.R.E.*, Chapters 6 and 10; see also references, particularly to R. M. Hare and R. S. Peters. (When I say 'I have argued . . .', of course plenty of other moral philosophers have argued along similar lines, often more competently. Few philosophers would deny that 'being reasonable about morals' means *something*, and something not too far removed from what I have said.)

educated, and inviting them to make use of the components to settle moral questions: that is, questions about what they ought to do. We may hope that this will itself help to develop the components in our pupils: but we are not here concerned to develop them in any indirect or covert way. We are, in effect, presenting them with morality as a coherent *subject:* analogous to, though in certain respects different from, other subjects which they learn at school.

By contrast, we may make all sorts of arrangements for the curricular content and social context of our school – having a house system, teaching the pupils to appreciate literature, impromptu acting, role-playing, voluntary service – which we hope will develop our pupils' qualities or skills: but here we are, in a sense, using *indirect* methods. To take an analogy: we may, indirectly, help our children to play football better by giving them special exercises, making them sprint, breathe deeply, etc.; but we can also help them directly and overtly by teaching them to play football as such – teaching them the rules, how to win, and how to settle particular tactical problems: what we might call the 'methodology' of football.

If this is in principle a possible and desirable enterprise, then it is one which can be undertaken in good conscience by all teachers, whatever their own particular beliefs or commitments in the area of moral and religious ideals. One would hope that *all* teachers were 'committed' to *some* set of moral principles, whether or not derived from religious or quasi-religious beliefs. There are those, however, who seem to suppose that their particular 'commitment' precludes their teaching the kind of thing we have described. For such, the following points may be helpful:

1. If the teacher thinks the moral methodology we shall use is just *wrong* (logically in error) I cannot argue with him here, but would again simply ask him to refer to the relevant literature.[1] It may however help some teachers to be reminded that the methodology is emphatically *not* based on some particular or partisan 'faith', 'creed', or set of values (that might be labelled 'humanist', or 'utilitarian', or whatever). Those who, consciously or unconsciously, use it to solve their own moral problems would come (I should guess) from all 'faiths' or 'creeds', from humanists, atheists, or any other group. The methodology is based (it will be remembered) in an analysis of what it means to be *reasonable* in the area of morality; and I should hope that there will be few

[1] See book references on pp. 151–2.

teachers who would have little or no commitment to being reasonable, and to helping their pupils to be. If the reader has no such commitment,[1] I fear this book is not for him.

2. If on the other hand he thinks that, because of his own particular moral views, he cannot be properly neutral in such teaching, then this is just a muddle. For exactly the same consideration applies to any form of teaching. I may have my own preferences in English literature (I admire Milton and dislike Shelley): but this does not prevent me from educating pupils to read critically and intelligently – for educating them does not mean persuading them to share, or reject, my own particular views. Similarly my own particular historical views do not preclude me from the educational task of trying to make my pupils better historians. In other words, the teacher cannot of course be neutral in the sense of having no particular beliefs of his own: but he is not required to be neutral in that sense. For in the educational process his particular beliefs function merely as subject-matter, perhaps to be compared with other particular beliefs, but certainly not to be sold to (nor withheld from) the pupils.

3. Any teacher worth his salt will be too interested in helping the pupils to make up their own minds to be seriously worried by his own 'commitments'. For that is what education is about. Provided he has a prior 'commitment' to reason, truth and clarity, which overrides his own particular beliefs – and if he has not, then he should not be a teacher – he has no need to trouble himself unduly over this problem.

A. ADVANTAGES AND OBJECTIONS

Before considering why this method is controversial, I shall claim some important advantages for it:

1. First, it is *honest*. If we suppose that we are in a position to educate pupils morally at all, then we thereby claim to have some idea about the aims of moral education: about the qualities required by people for settling moral problems reasonably: and about how those qualities should be deployed. That is, we claim some knowledge of morality as a subject, and of the methodology appropriate to it. If we do not claim this, we have no right to be in business at all. But if we do, then it is dishonest and stupid

[1] See *E.R.E.*, pp. 1–6.

to conceal it from our pupils. It would be as if we were scared of laying before our pupils the subjects of science, history, and mathematics *as* subjects, together with the methods of procedure appropriate to each, and tried only to give them the necessary skills and techniques by some indirect means.

The point is not that it is always right to tell pupils the truth (though it nearly always is). The point is that, if we do not approach our pupils directly in this matter, we are not treating them as rational creatures at all. Moral education will be merely one more case of educators *doing things to* pupils, without telling them what the point and purpose of these are, and hence – inevitably – without enlisting their cooperation as co-equal, if more ignorant, human beings. The pupils will again be on the *receiving end* of a vast and heterogeneous number of practices whose purposes are known only to the educators. The psychological effects of this would repay research: but we can see *a priori* that they are not likely to be beneficial. At best, the pupils will be uncertain about what they are supposed to be trying to *do :* they will be confronted by no clear aims and objectives. At worst, the uncertainty may for some pupils turn into an intense anxiety, almost a mild paranoia; the teachers' objectives in moral education, because not spelled out to the pupils, become regarded as sinister, untrustworthy, 'authoritarian', 'indoctrinatory', and so forth.

It seems to me, therefore, extremely important to make it absolutely clear to pupils what we, as educators, are trying to do in moral education, and how to tackle morality as a subject. This would remain true, I think, even if our objectives were partisan – to produce good Communists, or good Catholics, or to force certain other specific moral beliefs and practices onto our pupils. But it is particularly relevant if our objectives consist, as they do, rather in helping people to think and act more reasonably for themselves. We need to get it across to the pupils that we are not out to force them into any kind of mould.

2. Secondly, it is *professional*. By this I mean that we ought to, and now can, get well beyond the stage of merely 'discussing moral problems', 'arousing concern', 'stimulating interest', 'being open-ended', and so forth. A lot of (no doubt useful) work has been done along these lines: but so many educators nowadays are scared of being thought 'authoritarian' that they give their pupils no clear idea that there are *right and wrong answers* to moral

problems: that there is a coherent *methodology* for settling them. This inevitably creates, or reinforces, a feeling very common today, not only amongst the young: the feeling that is sometimes expressed in such words as 'It's all relative really, isn't it?', 'It's just a matter of how you feel', 'Different people have their own views', 'It's a matter of taste', etc. Just as, in science or other subjects, it is one thing to encourage and help pupils to find out the answers, and the reasons behind the answers for themselves, but quite another to imply that there *are* no answers: so in morality the 'open-endedness' or 'child-centredness' of the discussion must not be allowed to obscure the fact that we discuss in order to find the truth – and hence that there is truth to find.

This can only be done by a direct approach; and it is better to err on the side of naivety rather than on the side of vagueness. Of course there are all sorts of philosophical problems about morality, just as there are problems in the philosophy of science and the philosophy of history. But there is nevertheless a coherent methodology which has as much right to be called reasonable, and to be learned by our children, as the methodologies of science, history and any other established subject. There will always be plenty of opportunity for discussion of more complex and sophisticated problems: what is important is that the children should be presented with this methodology in as professional a way as possible.

3. Thirdly, it *gives the children something to hang on to*. I avoid here the use of words like 'ideal', 'creed', 'faith', etc. precisely because we are not out to give them any *specific* set of moral or meta-physical beliefs. What we are trying to give them is something far more important, for which 'methodology' is as good a word as I can think of. We are trying to show them *how*, as rational creatures, they can identify and solve moral problems: just as, again, in science we show them *how* to answer questions about the nature of the physical world. It would be comparatively easy, and comparatively worthless, merely to *give* them our own answers (which may be wrong) in either case. But at the same time, we are giving them something: namely, a methodology. This is something which they can and must hang on to.

'Can', although it is difficult, and children (like adults) often prefer quick second-hand answers: 'must', because it is just as bad to give them nothing as to give them something second-hand. All the 'open-ended' discussions in the world do not amount to a methodology: they may do nothing more than dress up the pupil's vagueness and relativism in fashionable clothes. In the course of such discussions (and also in the course of other supposedly 'morally educative' activities, such as voluntary service, or going to chapel, or playing games, or whatever), any pupil with any guts is going to say to himself – and, I hope, to the teacher – something like 'Yes, this is all very interesting, but how do you tell what is *right*?' He will say this in all areas where the teachers do not put a clear methodology before him: in the area of morality, and (even more notoriously) in the area of religion. And if there are not many pupils with 'guts', in this sense, then there certainly ought to be.

Much has been said about the 'moral vacuum' left by the anti-authoritarian trend of the last few decades (and earlier): and of course it is right to point to the anxiety, the neurosis, the alienation, the drifting, the sense of being lost, that our pupils will have unless they are given something to hang on to. But it is also important, for the general future of education, that morality as a coherent subject is not allowed to perish by default. This is something which could well happen to religion: because people are not clear, nor agreed, about a methodology appropriate for settling questions in the religious area, we may easily relapse into a form of education where the *truth* (if any) or *merit* of religious beliefs is simply not tackled at all, or tackled only by those pupils who choose to tackle it. If this did happen to religion, and/or to morality, it would be a major disaster. We should have given up the whole idea of *education* in these fields, because we should have given up the whole idea of what is true or false, right or wrong, appropriate or inappropriate; and this could have far worse long-term consequences than anything which happens to the pupils immediately under our care. We have to give them something to hang on to: and we have to hang on to it ourselves.

Why, then, should this 'direct method' be a matter of controversy? There are a number of rather vague notions which seem to tell against it, which I shall deal with in turn:

1. First, it is sometimes thought that, since morality (unlike science, history and some other subjects) is concerned with behaviour and action, not just thinking, classroom periods are inappropriate: that an 'academic' approach to a 'practical' subject is mistaken. But nobody wants to say that pupils do not need *other* methods of

moral education – of course they do; or that these should not be 'practical' – of course they should. Nobody disputes that these other methods – what is done by way of curricular arrangements, the social life and structure of the school, personal contact with a certain type of teacher, and so on – may well do very much more to develop the moral components than can be done by the use of the direct method in the classroom. But this does not show the direct method to be unimportant. It is a disputable question how much 'theory' as opposed to 'practice' we need in morality: how much morality is like (say) learning to swim, where 'theory' is not very helpful, or how much it is like more strictly 'academic' subjects such as history or mathematics. But, for reasons which I made clear elsewhere,[1] *some* 'theory' is necessary. Morality is not *just* a matter of practice and habit. So the importance for moral education of the general life of the school, of pupil-teacher relations, or of any other indirect method, must not be allowed to count against the importance of a direct approach.

2. Secondly, some people have the idea that to teach this methodology would be appropriate only for older or very intelligent children. Perhaps they think that to discuss morality as a subject would necessarily involve a prolonged study of the more profound moral philosophers, and react against the (unnecessary) picture of explaining Aristotle and Kant to the fifth form. This is a curious prejudice: we do not explain Rutherford and Einstein to the fifth form either, but this does not tempt us to say that science is only suitable for clever boys or sixth formers. Or they may think that morality as a subject requires a kind of very difficult 'abstract reasoning' which is beyond the grasp of the average pupil. But this is not so: and it is fairly clear from the results of research that some, at least, of the types of reasoning required are well within the grasp of quite young children.[2] If we consider the moral components one by one, we shall not think it too rash to say, on general or *a priori* grounds, that the vast majority of children, even within the primary school age-range, will be capable of understanding each individually, and of understanding how they all relate to one's eventual moral behaviour.

This prejudice may be only one instance of a more general

[1] See *I.M.E.*, Chapter 1.
[2] See Norman Williams, 'Children's Moral Thought', in *Moral Education*, Vol. I, nos. 1 and 2 (Pergamon Press, Oxford), with references; also Norman and Sheila Williams, *The Moral Development of Children* (Macmillan).

bewitchment with the notion of certain studies as necessarily very 'high-powered' or 'academic'. What we call 'philosophy', 'psychology', or 'sociology' may be among these. A phrase like 'moral philosophy' is apt to put many people off: surely, they think, this is something which can only be done by Oxford dons. But if these titles stand for basic forms of thought – thought about language and concepts, about the minds and feelings of individual human beings, and about human society – it is in the highest degree unlikely that even young or stupid people could have absolutely *no* chance of learning them. In fact, of course, everybody does think, more or less competently, in these areas: everybody has some (however unformed) views and beliefs which could be fairly described as philosophical, psychological and sociological: or even if they did not, it would not be beyond the wit of man to teach them, so long as we are not frightened by the grandness of the mere *words*.

3. Thirdly, it is thought that we cannot teach the methodology of morality as a subject, because we are not clear or not agreed on what that methodology is. Here I cannot say very much that I have not said elsewhere. If there are (as, alas, there seem to be) people who think that we should settle moral matters by doing what the Church, or the Communist Party, or our peer group, or our guilt-feelings, or 'faith' or 'intuition' or fashion tells us: that some methodology of this kind, rather than that which we have outlined elsewhere, is what we ought to inititate our children into: and that this would be fairly called moral *education* – to such people I can only issue an invitation to consider or reconsider the relevant arguments.

4. Another sort of objection is somewhat more nebulous, but seems to consist in regarding morality as somehow too 'pure', or 'spiritual', or 'spontaneous', to be taught. Thus the idea of having *examinations* in moral thinking seems to some intolerable; and the idea of teaching pupils 'the right answers', which they then repeat to us, seems to degrade the whole concept of morality and moral virtue. However, this is just a muddle. Of course we shall not catch very much of our pupils' 'inner lives' in this particular net: and only an idiot would suppose that, in examining a pupil's grasp of the methodology of morality, we are thereby examining him as a virtuous *person* – qualifying or disqualifying him for the Kingdom of Heaven. Further, it should be unnecessary to add that we do not teach 'the right answers', but a

methodology for the pupil's own use – just as with any other subject. Only someone with a very curious outlook, who felt that moral decisions should not be rational at all, could sustain this objection.
5. Finally, there are various arguments which may be described as 'political' in a wide sense of the word. It may be thought unwise to put 'morality' or 'moral education' on the school time-table for various reasons, e.g. (a) the title will put students off, (b) it will be taken as a substitute for religious education, (c) it will suggest that this is *all* the school needs to do about moral education (see 1. above), (d) it will be unacceptable to parents, or adherents of particular creeds, or some other group of people, (e) who is to teach these periods? – and so forth. Of course all these points are important. Students must not be put off, the purpose of the teaching must be explained, various groups must be placated, teachers must be trained. But none of these points has very much to do with the question of whether, as a piece of *education*, such teaching would be valuable to our pupils. If so, and if we have a fairly clear idea of what it should consist of, then we must do it: and naturally the *title* does not much matter. I should be inclined to call it something like 'Moral Thinking', since that seems the simplest and most honest phrase to represent the content of the periods: but others may prefer other titles.

These objections, then, seem ill-founded. Moreover, there is one necessity which it is very hard to see how anything except direct teaching can meet. This necessity is something that is logically required by the concept of a morally educated person. It is that such a person must not merely act or feel in a certain *way*, but that he must do so for certain *reasons*. For instance, it is not sufficient that a person should give money to the poor, or refrain from stealing, or feel affection for his wife: for he might do all these for inadequate, or even disreputable, reasons – he wants to ingratiate himself with somebody, or is frightened of getting caught, or is romantically obsessed. He must act and feel *for the right reasons*. He cannot do this unless and until he knows what the right reasons are, and has convinced himself that they *are* right: and he cannot get to know this unless somebody teaches it to him.

This is a simple point, but it has wide ramifications. For example, to develop our pupils' regard and concern for other people as equals means far more than merely enabling them to 'get on with' pupils of a different social class, or 'freeing them from prejudice' against negroes, Jews, or foreigners. This in itself goes no way towards giving them the *right reasons* for treating certain types of creatures as equals. We may in some sense persuade them, indirectly, that skin colour, or accent, or status should not matter, or merely accustom them to these differences: but this may simply result in their developing other kinds of 'class distinctions' (perhaps against adults, or fat boys, or ignorant people – the list is endless), unless we teach them what *does* matter, what the real reasons are in virtue of which people have equal importance. These are not to do with their being (in the biological sense) people, human beings, two-legged inhabitants of this planet, which would exclude intelligent Martians: they rest on the fact that certain creatures have wills, desires, purposes, and intentions, make free choices and use language. It is because of this that there are good reasons (which we must make plain to the pupil) for counting them as equals; and the pupil must learn to act from these reasons, not from other reasons.

I do not see how any pupil is likely to learn this, or to learn it as quickly and fully as we should wish, unless he is directly taught it: that is, unless the reasons are overtly pointed out to him. If they are not, he is much more likely to fall back on some mode of moral thinking which is not such hard work, but also not so rational. He will have to be taken step by step through the reasoning which necessitates each of the components, and how each of them must operate, consciously or unconsciously, as the background of any moral action. I am not saying that this understanding necessarily involves any very high intellectual ability: but it does involve direct teaching. If we can make such teaching effective, and by the use of other methods make it transferable to real-life situations, then we may save much time that we now spend on particular instances, such as 'class distinction' or 'race prejudice'. For if we can establish in the pupils' minds (and hearts) the *general principle*, together with its reasons, which lies behind such cases, we shall have armed him effectively to deal with the particular instances on his own: whereas if we do not, we shall do no more than constantly plug new gaps, and mend the tears in a garment which will only tear again somewhere else because it is not properly made in the first place.

B. AIMS AND METHODS

Some of the aims of this direct teaching I have already mentioned *en passant* in section A above:

1. To make our pupils understand that moral thinking, like scientific and other kinds of thinking, is a serious subject of study in its own right, and can result in right or wrong answers to moral questions: that there is a rational methodology: and thereby to provide them with the right reasons for moral action and feeling.
2. To give them (as it were) a psychological resource when confronted with moral situations in everyday life: neither selling them a partisan 'faith' nor leaving them in a vacuum, but initiating them into a technique which they can use for themselves in coping with real-life problems.

To these we can add somewhat different but closely-connected aims:

3. To induce, by constant practice, the actual *habit* of using this methodology, so that there is a better chance of their doing so in everyday life.
4. To wean them away from false methodologies (reliance on the peer group, on authority or 'anti-authorities', on false ego-ideals, and so on).
5. By clarifying the logic of the moral components, both individually and in their collective operation, to give them insight into which *particular* components are lacking, both in themselves and other people, in particular cases.
6. Hence, by making them aware of these deficiencies, to give them at least the chance of developing the components for themselves, and of welcoming any other studies or activities that would encourage such development.

We can claim on *a priori* grounds that the direct method would at least be likely to achieve these aims to some degree. This is, of course, *not* to make empirical claims about the degree of 'transferability': that is, about how much effect this direct teaching will have on the pupil's actual behaviour and feeling – or even on his moral thinking – outside the classroom. Nevertheless, although we badly need research in this area, this is not a good reason for disqualifying the direct method. For, first, it is unlikely that this teaching would have *no* effect outside the classroom: secondly, only a fool would fail to back it up by other methods (including those mentioned later in this book) which would encourage transferability: and thirdly, to have taught pupils how they ought to operate in the moral area is to have achieved something, even if they rarely do so: we do not normally object to teaching our pupils the truth merely on the grounds that they may not often make use of it.

In considering methods, one distinction needs to be made absolutely clear from the start. As the reader will have grasped already, we shall be teaching the pupils how they *ought* to think in the moral area. This is not to teach them about what they and others *do* think: it may be useful to bring in such facts by way of example, but this is not the purpose of the exercise. To use a parallel: when we teach scientific methods we are trying to show the pupil how he ought to think as a scientist, what procedures he ought to follow in order to answer scientific questions. To tell him about how most (ignorant) people actually *do* think or have thought – about those who think the earth is flat, or who believe in astrology, or who tried to settle questions of cosmology by reference to the scriptures – may be of incidental use, perhaps in pointing the contrast between these false methods and the properly scientific one. But our aim is not to give him such factual knowledge: our aim is to teach him to think as a good scientist ought to think.

This does not make the factual studies – the psychology, sociology, history, etc. of morals – unimportant. But it does mean that we must distinguish them sharply from what we might rather grandly call the 'normative' study of moral thinking – that is, the study of how one *ought* to think in the moral area. Here too there is a parallel with religion. It is one thing to study beliefs and practices of different religions and creeds as an end in itself – the sociology of religion, or 'comparative religion' – but it is quite another to study the principles by which one ought to assess or evaluate the *truth* or *worth* of such beliefs, which necessarily involves having a clear idea of how a rational person should make up his mind in the religious area.

In talking of the 'direct method', or of classroom periods labelled (perhaps) 'Moral Thinking', I am concerned only with the 'normative' study. It must be clearly understood that this, and not factual knowledge for its own sake, is the central aim. It would, I am sure, be highly profitable for pupils to learn something of the psychology, sociology and history of morals, both for its own sake and because it would provide useful material and examples for the normative study with which we are concerned. But this is a logically different kind of enterprise, and must be kept distinct – at least in the mind of the teacher, and I should guess also in our actual classroom periods. It will be difficult enough for the pupils to grasp the idea that they are supposed to be learning about how they ought to think – how it is rational to think – without confusing them by telling them, in the same classroom during the same period, about how people actually do think, unless it is quite clear to the pupils that this is merely being offered for the sake of example.

I do not want to enter a debate about details of teaching-methods, which can only be resolved by experimentation and research. But the teacher of 'moral thinking' must, at least, not allow himself to be carried away by fashionable talk of 'integration', 'breaking down the subject-barriers', and so forth. One of the chief points behind the whole of this 'direct method' is to put 'moral thinking' clearly and firmly on the map as a subject: to make it easily identifiable to the pupils, so that they do not confuse it with other types of study: to make quite sure that they are learning something (rather than merely being stimulated, or having their interest and concern aroused), and that they are learning *this* rather than something else. If we do not ensure this, there is little point in the operation at all. And, subject to research-findings proving the contrary, I should argue strongly that we need to keep these periods uncontaminated by other subjects.

This is by no means to say that highly effective methods might not be devised which could be called 'integrated' or 'interdisciplinary'. For instance, we could arrange that, in history or English lessons, or better still in lessons about psychology or sociology, the teachers dealt with material which was in some way relevant (if only as illustration) to the purpose of the 'moral thinking' periods. Or, if we want to be still more 'interdisciplinary', we could take a topic like 'sex': we devote some time to the biology of sex, some time to the psychology, some time to the sociology, or history, or whatever: and also some time to it in the 'moral thinking' periods, where our question would be 'How *ought* we to make decisions in the sexual area?' All this may be very desirable – so long as the distinctions between the disciplines are clearly preserved in the minds of the children. But since, to date, they are not even clear in the minds of most teachers, I should question whether most existing integrated or interdisciplinary courses of this kind were anything more than a (possibly stimulating) muddle. There are certainly no solid grounds, based on research, for adopting them; but of course every teacher must decide for himself.

We must also remember what was said at the end of section A about the chief aim of the direct method – to explain the proper *reasons* to the pupil, so that he has some chance of appropriating them for himself. This means that, whatever specific content we give to the 'moral thinking' periods, we must select it with this objective in mind. The pupil must, sooner or later, be able to *understand, state,* and *apply* the right reasons to relevant cases. This means that, at some stage, the medium of teaching and learning must be *words*. For the notion of having or understanding a reason is bound up with the notion of *saying* (or being in principle able to say) certain things to oneself and to other people: things of the form 'PQR are the case, therefore I should do X' ('So-and-so is a creature with desires and feelings like myself, therefore I should count his wants as of equal importance to my own').

All this may seem very 'abstract' and 'philosophical'. But it is not. I am simply pointing to the very important differences between a person who acts for no reason at all, or for the wrong reason, and a person who acts for the right reason. The former may, accidentally, do 'the right thing' out of habit, or impulse, or fear, or conditioning: only the latter will count as being 'morally educated' – and the test will be whether he is in principle able to show us that it was for *this* reason that he acted. He would have to *use* the right reason in his thinking and behaviour. Many of us are like the former person: we use the wrong reasons, or no reason at all, or we think we are using the right reason when really some other reason influences us. Perhaps the really 'morally educated' person – the person who has a genuine concern for others and uses that concern (and it only) in his actions towards others – is pretty rare. But this makes it all the more important to turn our pupils into this sort of person, in so far as we can. And we can only make sure that we are doing so by checking on what they *say*, and thereby on what is really going on inside their heads.

The relevance of this to the specific content is obvious. Of course we shall not teach them simply by *telling* them what the right reasons are and getting them to repeat the reasons. Probably we should then get only parrotted answers. We must show them the existence and proper application of such reasons in various contexts and illustrative examples: and the more 'real' the contexts and examples are, the better. As far as possible, we must bring the contexts close to real-life decisions, and we must be open to the use of any method which will do the job. We may think here not just of using modern, 'with-it' examples, but also of such methods as acting, role-playing, simulation-situations, the use of films, tape-recordings, video-tape, and so on. Perhaps it will be desirable to take the children out of the classroom and introduce them to situations in the outside world: or in the actual running of the school: or in their own homes. A competent and imaginative teacher (particularly if he follows the 'progressive' fashion) will not need me to tell him about such methods. But – and it is a big 'but' – these methods must be geared to getting the pupil to understand, *in language*, the reasons we have been talking about: and this is a far cry from merely 'stimulating interest' or 'arousing concern'.

C. EXPLAINING THE 'MORAL COMPONENTS'

It is possible to approach the methodology of morality by various routes;[1] and I do not want to suggest that the methodology which follows is the *only* possible, or the only valuable, approach. Much might be gained, for instance, by making and examining a list of the moral virtues (truthfulness, courage, etc.), and developing classroom periods on these lines. Nevertheless, for reasons given more fully elsewhere,[2] I think there are very strong arguments for using a methodology based on the 'moral components', which I mentioned briefly earlier; they are listed more fully below, and defended in previous works.[3] They have, at least, the merits of clarity, simplicity and coherence. It is essential that the teacher should avoid vague, 'global' terms like 'sensitivity', 'maturity', 'awareness', 'an adult attitude', and so forth: these sound well, but mean nothing specific enough to form a basis for clear instruction.

At the same time, the teacher must be aware that a number of very *different* things are required by the morally educated person. Indeed the attraction, and equally the danger, of the vague 'global' approach (in terms of 'maturity', etc.) is that it saves us the hard work of sorting out these different things. But from this there is no escape, either for ourselves or our pupils: we, and they, must be prepared to work at it. The 'technical terms' – PHIL, EMP, and so on – are not merely jargon or unnecessary obscurity: they are required as clearly-defined titles for these logically different factors. The distinctions have to be made somehow: if they are not, the teaching and learning will simply not get done. I make no apology, then, for using our own terminology and method of approach.

CONCERN FOR PEOPLE: PHIL (1) AND (2)
As I have tried to explain elsewhere,[4] PHIL is an attitude which

---

[1] Some of which I have described in *I.M.E.*, pp. 212–17.
[2] ibid., and *E.R.E.*, Chapter 6.
[3] ibid.
[4] *E.R.E.*, pp. 217–26.

may roughly be described as 'concern for (other) people as equals'. We distinguish, again roughly, between PHIL (1) or justice, which is a matter of respecting others, giving them their (equal) rights, etc. and PHIL (2) or benevolence, which goes further and is a matter of being able to make their interests part of one's own – to be happy in giving happiness to others. I shall not go through the arguments for PHIL more fully here.[1] What is important is to be sure that the pupil grasps the concept properly.

PHIL is an attitude: and we need to introduce our children to its separate parts:

(a) *Having the concept of a person* – understanding that the members of a certain class of creatures (those with consciousness, desires, language, etc.) are importantly similar.
(b) *Belief* – that other rational creatures *are* our equals and worthy of respect and consideration as such.
(c) *Feeling* – the feeling of respect, or benevolence, which should normally accompany the belief.
(d) *Action* – the action taken to help others, or avoid harming them, which would normally flow from the belief and the feeling.

It has to be made plain that a person may quite sincerely and genuinely be concerned for others, and hence have PHIL, but that this concern may sometimes be overridden by other beliefs and emotions. Thus I might be genuinely anxious to make friends with somebody and to be nice to him, but so nervous or frightened that I do not take the appropriate action; or a person in a totalitarian country might be sincerely concerned for the fate of an unfortunate minority group (say, the Jews in Nazi Germany), but too frightened to do anything about it because he might be killed himself if he did. These are cases where the *belief* is present, and also the *feeling* of concern; but where these, though genuine, are not overriding, and hence do not result in action. At the same time there are limits, and these are special cases. If a person said he was concerned with somebody, but rarely or never did anything to help him even when given a fair opportunity, we should soon come to doubt his sincerity.

Of these four elements, the direct-method teacher will be most concerned with (a) and (b). (a) in particular – having a proper concept of a person – lends itself most obviously to direct teaching: and it is remarkable how many pupils (and adults) either do not have this concept, or do not choose to apply it. 'Person' may mean to them

[1] ibid.

only creatures with white skins, or only the genus *homo sapiens*, or only grown-ups, or only those 'on our side'. We have somehow to get pupils to go behind the appearances to the crucial element of rational consciousness (perhaps this is what 'having a soul' might most usefully mean). Pupils must have and use the concept of a person as a source of wants and needs: after grasping this, it is fairly easy to see that one's own particular wants and needs are nothing special – that there is no reason for them to count any more than other people's.

The grasp of the belief-element (b) – that people count equally – of course goes closely with the feeling-element; we might go so far as to say that a person who had absolutely *no* feeling of respect or benevolence for other people could not really or sincerely believe that they were his equals and his brothers, or that they had needs and emotions just as he had. But the direct-method teacher will only be able to induce the appropriate feeling *via* explaining the belief and its reasons. He has got to convince (without browbeating) the pupil that, whatever one may or may not feel on particular occasions, all rational creatures *are* in fact our equals: that our instinctive feelings may be quite irrelevant to what we ought to feel and how we ought to act. By a judicious choice of examples and arranged experiences, 'monitored' and commented on *en courant* by the teacher, this point should not be too difficult to make. It is, after all, essentially the point vividly made by the parable of the Good Samaritan: and the imaginative teacher will be able to think of a great many ways of ramming it home.

But here again we must not let our examples and arranged experiences stray too far. It may be comparatively easy to get our pupils to feel and act in certain ways that *look* like PHIL-type ways. For instance, as we saw earlier, it may be easy to get them to feel concern for certain *classes* of people – perhaps those who are dependent or non-threatening, such as old people or very young children or those with physical handicaps. But it may be something special about these classes which encourages our pupils to have these feelings – their dependence, or their pitiable state: just as one may more easily feel affection for (say) cuddly, furry animals rather than for snakes or spiders. To be concerned for people, *qua* people (rather than *qua* attractive blondes or rich uncles), is much more difficult. Again, we may arouse the mere *feeling* – the rush of affection, pangs of conscience or whatever – without arousing genuine concern. They may simply want to express their instinctive affection, or

assuage their guilt-feelings, without much regard for the people as
such: just as one may feel very affectionate about a cuddly, furry
animal without actually being concerned about it (perhaps one
enjoys feeding it so much that it becomes ill).

Thus it is too easy to devise practical contexts or experiences
which may show the child *some* reason for adopting the attitude of
PHIL, but not the *right* reason. No doubt, for instance, it pays off
if we show respect and concern for others, in as much as they are
then more likely to show it to us: and we could easily arrange for
our pupils to have experiences (if enough do not exist already)
which will drive this point home – the bully gets bullied, the stealer
stolen from, and so forth. This may indeed be desirable, just as it is
desirable for pupils to know that (whether they have PHIL or not)
the law will punish them for theft. But it does not teach them PHIL
as such. The point of one of the earliest and most classic attempts
to educate a child morally – when the parent says 'How would *you*
like it if *your* toys were stolen?' (or whatever) – is not to threaten the
child with retribution, but to remind him that, in stealing, he is
affecting the interests of another human being like himself: a human
being who, because like himself, has as much right to happiness as
he has.

I have spent rather a long time on PHIL: partly because it is
perhaps the most important of the components, but partly also
because I wanted to hammer home the point about making it crystal
clear to the pupils what the *concept* is. This is possibly most important in the case of PHIL, because it is so easy to miss the mark:
but it is also important in the case of the other components, and I
should like the reader to bear this general point in mind when we
discuss them.

AWARENESS OF FEELINGS: EMP(1) AND (2)
EMP is an ability, the ability to be aware of feelings and emotions in
other people (EMP(1)) and in oneself (EMP(2)). This includes not
only awareness of present emotions, but also the ability to know
what emotions a person had in the past, or will have in the future,
or would have under certain circumstances. I use 'feelings and
emotions' here to exclude sensations (e.g. physical pain), but to
include what might more properly be called 'moods' or 'states of
mind' (happiness, depression, desire, etc.).

To know what emotion a person is feeling – to be able to say
correctly 'He is frightened', 'He is hopeful', etc. – involves being

able to correlate a number of things which form part of the concept of an emotion. We may list these:

(a) *Belief* – a person who feels fear (for instance) characteristically believes that the object of his fear is dangerous: one who feels proud believes that he has done something remarkable, or has some outstandingly good quality.

(b) *Symptoms* – every emotion has characteristic symptoms: thus a person who feels fear is liable to tense his muscles, perhaps turn pale or tremble; the angry man scowls, gets red in the face, etc.

(c) *Action* – many emotions naturally express themselves in certain ways: the frightened man flees, the angry man strikes out, etc.

(d) *Circumstances* – there are certain sets of objects or circumstances which characteristically inspire particular feelings: thus, dangerous objects inspire fear, delightful objects hope or desire, powerful or overwhelming objects awe, thwarting or opposing circumstances anger or impatience, insuperable difficulties despair, and so on.

We all learn, to some degree, to tell what emotions a person feels by one or more of these pieces of evidence: by guessing what somebody believes, noticing a facial expression or bodily posture, seeing what he does, or observing what circumstances he is confronted by. To develop EMP precisely is to develop this ability, which we all have to some extent. Some have it, but do not use it because they do not bring it to bear on actual situations (lack of KRAT(1)): none of us are as good at it as we ought to be. All this has to be explained to the pupil; we shall of course use examples, note our particular mistakes and the reasons for making them, discuss the particular emotions in detail, and so forth. We may test ourselves by giving illustrations where (say) the belief and symptoms are observable, but the actions and circumstances not observable, to see if we can induce the latter from the former: and other illustrations *vice versa*. We may consider the ambiguity of some symptoms ('Is X angry or merely depressed?'), the different kinds of actions people who feel a particular emotion may take (some run when frightened, others are rooted to the spot), and the peculiarly interesting case of irrational emotions, where the belief does not seem to fit the feeling (a person frightened of spiders which he knows to be harmless).

We shall want to go on to consider the peculiar difficulties of self-awareness (EMP(2)). In our own case, we are sometimes in certain respects well-placed, because we usually know what it is that

B

we believe and feel. But not always. We may easily be deceived ('I'm *not* angry!!' shouts the enraged man). We have a vested interest in concealing certain emotions even from ourselves: other people may perceive them more readily, from our symptoms and actions, even though they cannot get inside our skins. It is perhaps the more disreputable emotions, or the emotions we are frightened to face, that we deceive ourselves about: feeling guilty, feeling small and impotent, feeling full of hate. These problems have been discussed elsewhere.[1]

This will lead us to make a rough distinction between the application of EMP, both in the case of other people and of ourselves, to (a) conscious emotions and (b) unconscious ones. A person's ability may operate very well for the more obvious, surface-level emotions that he and others have: but he may be very bad at going deeper, at detecting what it is that he and others 'really' or 'unconsciously' feel. Thus a parent may see readily enough that his teenage son appears angry with him, but not have sufficient insight to realize that underneath this anger (and not very far underneath) there is a good deal of anxiety and uncertainty about his own strength and status. There are emotions which rest on unconscious beliefs, which people do not admit even to themselves: to detect these, insight is required.

It may be useful to formalise these types and applications of EMP thus: EMP(1) (a) – Conscious; EMP(1) (b) – Unconscious; EMP(2) (a) – Conscious; EMP(2) (b) – Unconscious. We could choose examples to illustrate all these, and pupils may practise them 'in the field': on their friends, their families, literary illustrations, and so forth. Here again I shall not try to do the teacher's job for him by suggesting methods in detail. So long as he remembers to choose his examples and methods by relating them to the different *conceptual* points about EMP made here, so that the pupils grasp the whole of the concept, he will do very well.

FACTS AND KNOW-HOW: GIG(1) AND (2)

GIG is an attainment: it is concerned with knowledge (excluding awareness of emotions, which merited the separate component EMP). We distinguish between GIG(1) and GIG(2). GIG(1) is knowledge of the hard facts relevant to moral situations: that is, to situations where important interests are at stake. A person with adequate GIG(1) will know, for instance, that certain drugs are addictive, that fast driving is liable to be dangerous, that certain

[1] *E.R.E.*, Chapter 9.

methods of contraception will prevent unwanted children, and so on. In general he will know about:

(a) the laws, social norms and conventional expectations of society at large, and of the groups he is likely to mix with;
(b) basic facts concerning the physical health, safety and well-being of humans generally;
(c) facts concerning the needs and social position of particular groups, perhaps especially the underprivileged.

Of course this list, and its particular items, are indefinitely extensible: one never knows, so to speak, when a bit of GIG may not be useful for a moral decision. I mention here only the more straightforward examples, in order to make the concept (which is all the teacher is concerned with) clear.

GIG(2) is a matter of 'knowing how' rather than 'knowing that'. It is an element which cannot be reduced to factual knowledge, but consists rather in a kind of skill ('know-how') which can perhaps only be acquired by practice. Just as a person can know all the rules of cricket, and be very anxious to play it well, but nevertheless play very badly for lack of practice or natural flair: so in dealing with other people one may have plenty of PHIL and EMP and KRAT, and know all the relevant facts (GIG(1)), but still somehow be incompetent or *clumsy*. This may be particularly true of such a person in specific contexts: some people are no good at teaching because they cannot control a class, others are no good at giving clear commands, others again are gauche when it comes to expressing sympathy. Some of these failures, of course, may well be due to lack of some other component (perhaps particularly lack of EMP); but not all. There is an irreducible element of '*savoir faire*', of skill or knack or flair. This is GIG(2).

Illustrations of GIG(1) are easy: and it is not too hard to think of ways in which one can exemplify GIG(2) also (e.g. playing particular roles – a giver of orders, a bestower of sympathy, a person who wishes to express gratitude in a gracious way, etc.). The concepts here are not particularly hard to grasp.

NOTICING AND DECIDING (KRAT(1))

This component is concerned with *bringing to bear* one's PHIL, EMP and GIG on a particular situation. For one may of course in some sense *have* these other components – a general attitude of concern for others, the ability to know what they feel, and the relevant factual knowledge and 'know-how' – without actually *using* them or bringing them to bear.

We may divide KRAT(1) roughly into:

(a) *being alert to* a situation which calls for moral thought and action (not being wrapped up in a day-dream, too concerned with oneself, too anxious etc.);
(b) *thinking thoroughly* about the situation: that is, not making a merely superficial use of one's PHIL, EMP and GIG, but working it out seriously and patiently, so as to arrive at a decision about what one ought to do;
(c) *thinking responsibly* or 'prescriptively' about the situation: that is, reaching a decision not just that something should be done, but that *I ought* to do it. If I do this I *prescribe* the action for myself, or genuinely *commit* myself to it.

All these elements must be present if the person is to reach the stage of making a proper moral decision; that is, a decision based on the right reasons (PHIL) and taking all the relevant facts into account (EMP and GIG). Many people may lack (a), and not be alert to the situation at all: they drift, act on impulse, and fail to confront reality;[1] it is not that they make the wrong moral decisions, but rather that they do not make *any* decisions – not that they think wrongly, but that they just do not think at all. Others may lack (b), and think only superficially: they may take too much for granted, or fail to be honest with themselves and hence describe the situation in a way which suits them ('I was only getting my own back', 'He's a blasphemer and a nuisance to us Pharisees, never mind if he's innocent, kill him'). Others may lack (c), and whilst vaguely assenting to the proposition that 'something ought to be done' do not (as it were) *order* themselves to do it, so that such PHIL as they have is not overriding and does not issue in a settled decision.

This is one of the most important components, at least as important as PHIL (with which it is closely connected). It has to do with the general notion of rationality, of confronting and coping with the outside world: but its implications for morality are obvious. These implications are as great for decisions which affect only or chiefly ourselves as for decisions which affect the interest of others (see DIK and PHRON below). Of course there are a great many different ways in which a person may lack KRAT(1), which we refer to by such words as 'fecklessness', 'anxiety', 'self-centredness', 'lack of

[1] See Part II, pp. 34–42.

determination', 'lack of persistence', 'imprudence', and many others. Different examples used by the teacher will show up these differences: thus there is, empirically, a big difference between the person who is carried away by anger and the person who is too anxious or apathetic; but both will probably fail to bring their PHIL, EMP and GIG to bear on real-life situations. But here again the teacher's job is to make the *logic* of the component clear.

The teacher will need to be careful here in explaining the (fairly obvious) distinction between PHIL, EMP and GIG on the one hand, and KRAT(1) and (2) (see below) on the other. PHIL, EMP and GIG are all (to put it roughly) things which a person may *have* but not always, or even perhaps often, *use*. Thus one may have an attitude (PHIL) but not always show it or adopt it: one may have the ability to detect emotions (EMP) but not always employ it: one may attain to certain knowledge (GIG) but not make use of that knowledge in real life. On the other hand, KRAT is precisely concerned with whether a person does or does not actually use these things. It would be logically absurd to say 'He has KRAT but never uses it', just as if we said 'He has the quality of alertness (or determination) but never uses it'.

TRANSLATION INTO ACTION (KRAT(2))

A person, by bringing to bear (KRAT(1)), his concern, awareness of feeling, and factual knowledge (PHIL, EMP and GIG), will necessarily reach the stage of making a firm decision about what he ought to do. But he still may not do it. He may be too scared, too impatient, too selfish, too forgetful, etc. We require the component KRAT(2) to bridge the gap between decision and action, just as we required KRAT(1) to bridge the gap between concern, awareness, etc. and decision. A person who has KRAT(2), then, is a person who translates his decision into action.

There is nothing particularly hard in the logic of KRAT(2). Naturally the same empirical reasons (anxiety, etc.) may produce a lack of KRAT(2) as produce a lack of KRAT(1) – a person may be bad both at reaching a decision, and at carrying out such decisions as he has made, because he is over-anxious, bored, angry, etc. And these same empirical reasons may, for all we know, also account for lack of PHIL, EMP and GIG. It must be remembered that these are *logical* components, not empirical qualities. What psychological 'forces' actually produce, or militate against, the components is a very open question, and one with which the teacher is not here concerned.

The equation

As well as an understanding of each component, the pupil needs of course to grasp how, in correct moral thought and action, they fit together. The story is clear enough. A morally educated person has concern (PHIL), awareness of feeling (EMP), and relevant factual knowledge (GIG). He also brings these to bear on the actual situation (KRAT(I)), so that he makes a serious and responsible decision to act. He also has the motivation to translate his decision into action (KRAT(2)).

One addition is necessary here. Morality can be divided roughly into two areas: that in which other people's interests are at stake, and that in which a decision affects only or chiefly oneself. (PHIL is relevant to the first of these, but not directly relevant to the latter.) This distinction is sufficient to justify our marking the stage at which a person comes to a decision by two different terms, for which we use the words DIK and PHRON: DIK in relation to the area which concerns other people's interests, PHRON in relation to the other area, the area of personal prudence or personal ideals of life which do not directly affect others. It is worth using these terms, because the DIK- or PHRON-stage is a matter of great importance, and is worth considering in its own right. It has to be remembered, of course, that DIK and PHRON do not stand for components but for a stage in the process of moral thought and action.

With this addition our 'moral equation' is complete. It is when a person has brought his PHIL, EMP and GIG to bear, by means of KRAT(I), that he reaches the DIK/PHRON stage, at which he makes a firm moral decision. He then requires only KRAT(2) to produce the right action. This can be represented thus:

$$\left.\begin{array}{l} \text{PHIL}(\text{I}) \text{ and } (\text{2}) \\ \text{EMP}(\text{I}) \text{ and } (\text{2}) \\ \text{GIG}(\text{I}) \text{ and } (\text{2}) \end{array}\right\} + \text{KRAT}(\text{I}) \text{ lead to DIK/PHRON: DIK/PHRON} \\ + \text{KRAT}(\text{2}) \text{ lead to right action.}$$

This is, as we have said, not an equation representing 'psychological forces'; it is an equation representing what is *logically* required for 'morally educated' behaviour. Nor is it a chronological equation: the different components do not necessarily 'come in' in that *order*. Nor, finally, is it required that a person consciously and deliberately 'goes through' all the components in his mind before being able to act rightly. He must be acting for those reasons, and using these abilities and attainments; but this can be done unconsciously, or on the spur of the moment. Not all moral situations demand prolonged and consciously rational thought. To be rational in morality is to have these components: but it is not necessarily to *ratiocinate* a great deal.

The teacher will find that much profit may be gained by considering cases of moral misdoing, in order to detect which particular component is missing, and hence responsible for the error. (Of course there may be more than one missing.) In the misdemeanours of villains in western films, in our everyday misdeeds, in the faults of our friends, just what is it in each case that is lacking? Some cases, like that of the person who gives his aunt arsenic thinking it to be aspirin powder, are easy enough (lack of GIG(1)): others, like the case of Hamlet, are more difficult. It seems best to move from clear-cut illustrations to the more complex ones; and it is certainly mistaken to concentrate exclusively on moral *problems*, whether in our personal lives or (worse) in the public arena. For most moral situations are not *problematical* at all: there is usually not much doubt about the right answer. What we need is a series of straight-forward cases in our own everyday lives. If a person devotes most of his attention to complex and public-arena cases, it may well be a sign that he does not want to face the commoner cases that arise in his ordinary life (charity begins at home): and I would not recommend the discussion of difficult political or social issues, or of questions of foreign policy. We have to remember that our objective is to clarify the concepts and the methodology, not to conduct vague (if 'concerned') discussions about the welfare state or international relations.

Wrong ways of thinking
The teacher will inevitably have to deal with wrong (unreasonable, inappropriate) ways of thinking about morality, because these are very common among pupils – and adults. Indeed, his practical teaching might perhaps begin with a consideration of the various ways in which people make up their minds: that is, the *types of reasons* which they seem to use. From this he might go on to show the correctness of one way (the 'moral components', based on PHIL or concern for people's interests) and the temptations of other ways.

There is a good deal of research material the teacher can use here,[1] but the 'wrong ways' can be fairly simply categorized under three main headings:

(a) '*Other-obeying*'. This is the person who refers the question of

[1] See in bibliography under Kohlberg and Williams.

what he ought to do to some *outside authority* (what God or his
parents or the gang-leader says, what the Bible or Mao Tse-Tung
says, 'the code of the West', etc.).

(b) '*Self-obeying*'. This is the person who refers the question to some
inner feeling or picture of his own: for instance, to his feelings
of guilt or shame, or taboo-feelings, or his 'ego-ideal' ('what nice
girls/tough guys/English gentlemen/teenagers, etc. do').

(c) '*Self-considering*'. This is the person who refers the question to
his own advantage or benefit: whether he will be rewarded or
punished, gain or lose, improve or diminish his own position.

Following on from this, it will be useful to point out that very
often, when people give 'reasons' for their actions — 'Because God
says so', 'I just wouldn't feel right inside', 'It's just wrong', etc. –
they may not really be giving reasons in the sense of *justifications*
at all. They are, perhaps, not trying to show that their choice is right
or justified: they are just explaining it, or saying how they feel.
Anyone who is really concerned with *justification* will be more or less
bound to use another 'mode of thinking', the 'other-considering'
mode: this is the mode set out in full with our 'moral components'.
For justification must be based on the wants and interests of human
beings, considered equally. The trouble is often, not that people
reason incompetently or irrelevantly about morals, but that they
do not really try to reason or justify at all.

This in turn might be connected with the kinds of compulsions,
'raw' feelings and fantasies to which we are all subject, and which
are responsible for these pseudo-reasons. To A, certain things are
just taboo: B somehow feels he must behave as his peer-group behaves: C feels guilty or ashamed if he does not cut a certain kind of
figure: D feels compelled to follow some authority: E feels compelled to rebel against the authority: F just says 'What's in it for
me?'; and so on. A brief consideration of some area where *reasoning*
in terms of others' interests, is in fact extremely rare – say, the
sexual area, or the area of religious prejudice – will show pupils
clearly how easy it is for us to abandon reason altogether, and simply
echo our inner compulsions and fantasies.

EMOTION, RELIGION AND MENTAL HEALTH
Elsewhere[1] I have described and applied the moral components to
areas which, whilst still part of 'moral education' in a broad sense,

_____
[1] *E.R.E.*, *passim*.

are often described under such titles as 'education of the emotions', 'religious education', or 'mental health'; and there is a lot of work going on in schools which is supposed to relate to these titles. I shall not repeat all the points at length here; but, if this direct method is tried, it is important for the teacher to realize that he is dealing with a methodology and with concepts which apply more widely than to 'morality' in its narrower senses.

In our 'moral equation' we showed that the components produced the 'right action': but they should also produce the right *feeling* or *emotion*. Then (1) any serious talk about the 'education of the emotions', if 'education' be taken seriously and we are not simply talking about allowing pupils to let off steam or be 'creative', must necessarily proceed with these objectives in view. Again (2) in so far as anything that can seriously be called 'religious education' must concern itself with developing pupils' rationality in the sphere of religion, then it will be concerned with encouraging them to have the right emotions directed to the right objects in this sphere (e.g., perhaps, distaste for Hitler and admiration of Jesus). This means that such characteristically religious emotions as awe, reverence, guilt, love, etc. must be 'educated': and this in turn involves developing the components we have been discussing. Finally (3), in so far as 'mental health' is concerned with education, and not simply with tranquillizers and other drugs, social conditioning, brain surgery, glands, etc., then its objectives must again be to develop the components, which together make up part of what we mean by such phrases as 'sane', 'reasonable', or 'mentally healthy'.

The reader who wishes to go into this more fully should consult the relevant literature.[1] I mention it here because the question is bound to arise in the actual course of the 'moral thinking' periods, and because if the point is forgotten the teacher will be likely to isolate and seal off his teaching from other things that may be going on in the school. Thus what happens in the R.E. lesson, or in other periods that may connect with, or offer examples of, personal ideals based on the emotions, may be useful to the teacher as material: so too will any material in the field of 'mental health' or psychology. It is quite possible that the 'moral thinking' periods may be the *only* occasions on which our pupils are offered anything like an adequate methodology by which they can decide, rationally, for themselves; hence it is important to realize that this methodology is relevant to the areas I have mentioned, and not only to the more

[1] *E.R.E.* gives all the necessary references.

obvious and cut-and-dried area of interpersonal morality. For our pupils need more than a way of dealing with questions about stealing, sex, and bad behaviour in football stadia: if we pursue these examples too relentlessly, we are likely to bore them. They need also a way of answering the more general questions about life, questions more connected with the reasonableness or unreasonableness of what they *feel*, their emotions, than with what they *do*. If the teacher can make them understand this, both they and we will be saved a great deal of unprofitable talk – whether in the quasi-metaphysical language of 'ultimate concern', 'the meaning of life', etc., or in the jargon-ridden psychological language of 'adjustment', 'normality', 'maturity', and so forth.

It will not have escaped the intelligent and critical teacher that the vagueness and the jargon to which I have just referred is a sign that we have, so far, failed our pupils miserably in certain areas. All we seem able to do is either to retain a luke-warm authoritarianism, or else to talk at them in a 'progressive' but hopelessly incompetent and febrile way, in the hope that it will do some good. We can and must do better. In order to do better, we have to put this methodology before them *clearly*. I have throughout tried to stress clarity, and whilst of course teachers should be imaginative, lively, stimulating and so forth, I would place more stress on words like 'coherent', 'workmanlike', 'down-to-earth', and 'clearly articulated'. The vague, the metaphysical, the woolly, the high-sounding, and the woffly, must be avoided at all costs, however 'inspiring' or 'stimulating'. We need the clarity of the old authoritarian without his irrationality. Of course it is easy for a research worker to say 'This should be done', leaving the teacher to fill in the details and do all the work for himself.[1] But I am confident that all those teachers who see the point of this kind of teaching will be well able to make a good job of it.

---

[1] Though perhaps in self-defence, and also as an encouragement, I should add that I have taught such 'moral thinking' periods for ten years, through the 9–21 age-range, not without success.

PART II

Language and Communication

Human beings interact with each other in all sorts of ways, in many different kinds of social contexts, and with widely varying effects. All these may, in a very loose sense, be described as 'communication'. We may think of a classroom lecture, a discussion about drug-taking, a church service, a game of football, a tea-party, and so forth. Obviously all these are very different. One way of elucidating the differences is to use a metaphor or analogy which, though not exact at all points, is nevertheless useful: that is, to regard them all as different kinds of 'games' in which different sets of rules are (consciously or unconsciously) followed. This is not to say that they are not serious: it is rather to point to their *rule-governed* nature. The rules are in some cases very obvious, and may even be formalised, as for instance in real games, or in the rules of procedure which govern parliamentary and other debates, mock trials, and so on. In other cases the rules are tacitly acknowledged (even if sometimes broken): thus there are conventions governing what you say and do at a tea-party, or a church service, just as there are for playing chess or cricket, even though the rules may be less obvious or less easy to state clearly.

Our interest in these communication-games is to see whether one or more of them might contribute effectively to the development of one or more of the components that go to make up a 'morally educated' person. Plainly a great many 'games' or interaction-situations might improve some or all of the moral components; but it would be too big a task, in one book, to consider all the possibilities. I want to concentrate our attention on one component which seems very important: KRAT(1). We are here talking about whether a person (a) is alerted to a particular situation, and recognizes that there is something which he should stop and think about: (b) actually thinks thoroughly and effectively about it: (c) thinks responsibly and seriously about it, so as to end up with making a decision which commits him to acting in a particular way or advocating a particular view or course of action (the DIK-stage).[1]

The importance of KRAT(1) is considerable, because it seems likely that many people (perhaps particularly children and teenagers) are strikingly deficient in this component. There are no doubt some people who have little or no PHIL (concern for others): and some who have no idea about other people's feelings (EMP), or the 'hard' facts of a situation (GIG). But I should guess that there are far more whose fault is, not that they think incompetently or immorally, but that *they do not stop to think at all*. They act on impulse, drift, get carried away by the people they are with or by their own feelings, and so forth: they do not plan, form policies, think about the future, consider the effects of what they might do, or face the possibility of alternative actions. And it is not much use developing their PHIL, EMP and GIG if they never bring these components to bear because they lack KRAT(1).

In this Part of the book, therefore, we shall be concerned with one particular type of communication-game which seems *prima facie* likely to develop KRAT(1). But before considering it more fully as a teaching-method, it is very important that we should be clear exactly what it is that we are trying to develop here, and why it is plausible to connect it with the notion of communication. For the game we shall concentrate on is specifically a *language*-game: we shall be trying to develop something which we will call 'using language' in children, and we need to see why this 'using language' is crucial to KRAT(1).

A. 'USING LANGUAGE'

The importance of language to moral education cannot be understood unless the importance of language is first understood in itself. All teachers are in fact concerned with this area: either as teachers of English, or as teachers of some foreign language, or as helping children to express themselves orally or on paper, or just as instructors who have to rely on language in order to instruct at all. In all these areas, children may gain particular or 'local' benefits from language-teaching; and these benefits are easy to describe and well understood by all – 'to be able to make oneself understood in France' 'to enjoy German novels', 'to give a clear answer in an examination', 'to speak with a good accent', 'to acquire a wide vocabulary', 'to

[1] See pp. 25–27.

write a proper letter', and so forth. None of these objectives are to be despised; but they have little to do with moral education. We must probe deeper.

It will be best to proceed by listing a number of things with which the moral educator is *not*, or not primarily, concerned in the area of language:

1. Eloquence.
2. Immediate fluency.
3. A wide vocabulary.
4. 'Correct' grammar and spelling, accent, pronunciation, etc.
5. 'Self-expression' in the form of poetic or 'creative' writing.
6. Competence in *a particular* language.
7. The ability to detect linguistic fallacies (in propaganda, advertising, etc.).
8. The history of language, philosophy, etymology, etc.
9. An appreciative response to poetry and literature.
10. Wide reading.

Let me say at once that the above are far from unimportant: and also that the child who is educated to 'use language' in the way I want to describe will, almost certainly, display some (perhaps most) of the above as *symptoms* or signs that he has been so educated. But I would like to persuade the reader not to make a premature identification of 'language' with any or all of the above aims, but to clear the decks of his mind for a somewhat different approach.

By 'language' I shall mean the intentional use of conventional signs, of which words are only one example. (One might communicate by semaphore, gestures, flashing lights, or any other agreed and understood method.) What is central to language is that meaning is expressed by convention, by following certain agreed rules, as in playing a game. This use of signs is not confined to communication with other people: we employ it also within our own minds. It is called thinking. When we think (in a strict sense of the word, as opposed to feeling, day-dreaming, having mental images, and so forth) we *talk* to ourselves, as it were. We may not be conscious of doing so, and many of our actions, originally learnt by thinking, may now be habitual. But if asked, we would normally be able to explain in words what had gone on in our mind even in these cases. Our thoughts may move very quickly; but if they are really thoughts, and not just impulses, then they will be in some sense concerned with dealing with the outside world by this use of signs –

recognising things in it, putting it in order, solving problems in it, and so on.

Our ultimate concern is with forms of communication that may help children to carry out this process more effectively, and in particular help them to become more aware and conscious of the process itself. The importance of this will be obvious. For language, in the sense we are describing, is not just *one* useful tool that man has (in the way that he has fingers on his hands or uses screwdrivers): it is the way in which not only man but any conscious and intelligent creature deals with the world, instead of just reacting to it as animals do. It is not accidental, but an integral part of being conscious, rational and human that we use language. It is logically bound up with thinking, having reasons for our behaviour, and being responsible for our actions.

For much the same reasons, language is also logically bound up with moral thought and action.[1] Without language, there could be no such thing as morality, as there is no such thing as morality among animals. The morally educated person faces the world in general, and other people in particular, as a rational being, with concepts and language. He has purposes and achieves them: he is not merely pushed around by internal impulses or external pressures. This is not to say that he must be thinking, or talking, or ratiocinating all the time: it is just to say that he must be responsible for his actions – that his actions must be intended, and be in accordance with the rules and principles that make up morality. This has little to do with eloquence, less with 'creative writing', and practically nothing at all with grammar.

These few points about language should make it easy to appreciate the dangers inherent in three fashionable viewpoints, which are worth a brief criticism here if only because they will help to clarify our main points:

I. THE DOWN-WITH-WORDS MYTH

This is a popular myth to the effect that the medium of language (particularly written language) can be superseded by other media, such as visual images, sounds, textures, and so on. Like most myths, it rests on failure to observe a relevant distinction: the distinction between the use of objects (a) as conventional signs, and (b) for other purposes.

The word 'communication' is apt to blur this distinction. If I

[1] See *I.M.E.*, Chapter I.

affect people in various ways – by shouting, playing music, painting, reading poetry, or doing a strip-tease in front of them – there is no doubt a sense in which I am communicating with them: that is, I am making them *feel* something – perhaps the same sort of thing that I feel. I might make you feel horror and pity by showing you a photograph of a leper colony, or give you the rather more complex feelings that are 'communicated' by poems and other works of art. Here I do not use conventional signs – or if I do, I do not use them *as* conventional signs: I use potent symbols skilfully put together. I am not *telling* you anything, or stating facts, or describing, or representing the world as it is: my intention is to make you feel something about the world. On the other hand, if I use conventional signs as such, my interest is primarily to get something across to you, unemotionally and accurately. I have no interest in using these signs as potent symbols: no interest, that is, in selecting those signs that will work on your feelings.

These are two different jobs. One is not better or more respectable than the other: they are just different – somewhat in the way that prose is different from poetry, explanation from propaganda, and drawing accurate ordnance survey maps from sketching the outlines of an imaginary country in a way that will look pretty when hung on the wall. With the second of these, the symbolic or poetic use of language, we shall not be here concerned: how far this is relevant to moral education is an open question, about which the reader may inform himself elsewhere. We are concerned simply to show that the first – the conventional-sign use – is in principle irreplaceable.

In principle: for it could conceivably happen that human beings gradually lost interest in such rational activities as imparting information, learning facts, weighing probabilities, solving problems, following rules, and so on and that they simply reacted emotionally or aesthetically to various symbols – gaudy posters, sounds, images on the TV screen, etc. Whether we are witnessing the beginning of this process or not is a question of fact which sociologists must decide. In view of the apparent increase in reading and information-gathering throughout the world, perhaps it is unlikely. The point here is simply that the conventional-sign job cannot in principle be replaced by the other job, just because they are different. No amount of feelings about, or emotional or aesthetic responses to, various images or sounds can *tell* me anything, or solve any problems for me. It may inspire and motivate me, arouse my interest, raise my passions, or refine my artistic sensibilities: but it cannot think for me.

Hence we must not fall victim to a well-meaning but muddled attempt, on the part of some *avant-garde* educators, to 'replace the dry, conventional signs of informative prose and description by the living, creative flow of charged symbols', to 'allow the child to write as he feels, not to bore himself and us by merely factual description', or to 'help students to make up their own rules for language, instead of slavishly copying ours'. Of course images, symbols, poetry, free and 'creative' writing have an important part to play: if this were not so, we should have no business teaching poetry and literature at all – nor any of the other arts. But we need to repeat that the conventional-sign use of language is not *just another* skill (which might, for instance, quite well be replaced by woodwork or abstract painting). It is the mark, and the characteristic mode of being, of all rational creatures.

This does not mean that the two different jobs – the two different types of 'communication' – are wholly independent of each other, or need be practised independently. Quite the contrary. Learning may well proceed by a person first being emotionally moved, and then wanting to find out more about what moves him. For instance, a TV programme might begin with some shots of starving refugees, or old people suffering from poverty, or an outbreak of gang warfare: it might then move into the quite different realm of trying to discover, and tell the viewers, exactly what is happening and why – how many refugees are starving, why they are starving, what could be done and so on. Those in control of visual media may perhaps be tempted to place more stress on the former rather than the latter task, because the former is much easier. It is much harder work, both for the producers and for the viewers, to *think about* what is happening, and why, than simply to be moved by particular images.

What the teacher has to do is not to try to replace thinking by feeling, the conventional sign by the emotive symbol, but to persuade his pupils to progress from feeling into thinking – from being moved emotionally or aesthetically into solving problems. Perhaps all that the *avant-garde* educators really want to say is that the feeling must come first, otherwise not much thinking is likely to get done and of course this is true. We all know that motivation is very important in education. But it must not be confused with education itself. Pupils must want to learn: but wanting is not learning.

2. THE NUMERACY MYTH

It is, or used to be, commonly believed that 'numeracy' is as important as 'literacy': or, more generally, that it is just as important for pupils to learn how to do mathematics and (perhaps) science as it is for them to learn how to read, write and talk. Various arguments have been put forward for this – the importance of mathematics and science in the modern world, the gap between the 'two cultures', and so forth. I do not know whether these arguments are convincing, because the view they are supposed to support seems to me, as it stands, incoherent: and incoherent in a way which is very relevant to our understanding of the importance of language.

If 'literacy' were to include only such things as correct grammar and spelling, the ability to read and write simple English, and so forth, then this view would be understandable and perhaps defensible. There would be a number of rule-governed activities, not unlike games, into which we could initiate children: the English-language-and-grammar game, the arithmetic-game, the formal-logic game, the Latin-translation game, and so forth: teaching these would be not unlike teaching children to play chess, Monopoly, Scrabble, crossword-games, etc. It might then reasonably be claimed that the mathematics-game happened to be extremely useful for dealing with the physical world as we know it, and that it was at least as important for children to be able to play this game as for them to be able to make up Latin verses in the style of Ovid (to mention one very game-like activity).

However, it is part of our thesis (whatever may be meant by the word 'literacy') that language is not identified with any particular language (e.g. French) or rule-governed activity or game (e.g. Euclid or chess). Teaching linguistic skills to pupils is not teaching them English: though teaching them English may be one way of teaching them linguistic skills. Indeed it is misleading of me to talk here of 'linguistic skills', as if we were trying to produce good interpreters or good debaters or orators. Our concern is to make the child more rational by helping him to use some – any – language to deal with himself and the world: it is not to give him facility in any particular specialized language or languages.

Perhaps an example will help to clarify this: suppose the child, whether he knows it or not, is faced by a particular problem: say, how to get on with a rather bad-tempered father. If he is good at language, in our broad sense of the term, he will not just hit out at his father, or sulk, or run away: he will start asking himself questions, seeking facts, trying to find solutions, and in general *saying something to himself*. He will say, for instance, 'Oh, dear, father is angry again.

I wonder why: has he had a bad day at the office, or has he got a headache, or what? I'd better ask him and find out. Meanwhile is it best to keep out of his way, or try and cheer him up?', and so forth.

Now in order to solve his problem he may need certain *particular* linguistic skills, or knowledge of particular disciplines: perhaps he needs to have some social skill in addressing older people: or perhaps it would help if he knew a lot about how to cure headaches, or about the psychology of anger, or whatever. These specialized languages or fields of knowledge are often relevant: but they are not the first step, nor the most important step.

Getting the child to take this first step – to use a linguistic/rational approach – must be done, however, in the context of, or *via*, a particular language. The child has got to think in some symbols, and use some conventional signs: and obviously the most appropriate and useful signs are those of the child's natural language – in this country, the English language. We call languages like English and French 'natural' languages precisely because they are those languages in which people naturally and habitually think. Other languages or quasi-languages, like mathematics, are artificial and designed to solve particular problems: natural languages are the jumping-off point for solving *any* problem. So there is a sense in which English is more important than mathematics or (for the English child) any other language; because, in so far as the child is already thinking, he is thinking in that language.

3. THE LOGICIANS' MYTH

One very different school of thought needs mentioning, again chiefly because it will help to clarify our problem. It may be represented as follows: 'People often think illogically. They contradict themselves, and commit fallacies. They are swayed by propaganda, loaded words, and bogus arguments. If we teach them the nature of logic, explain various fallacies to them, etc., then they will know how to think rationally and avoid all the pitfalls.' Hence, in some schools, classes are conducted on these lines, and various books are used to try to help students 'think logically'.[1]

It is not (I hope) a myth to suppose that this kind of teaching is useful. But it is a myth to suppose that the central difficulties can be overcome by such methods. This picture again assimilates learning

[1] E.g. Susan Stebbing, *Thinking to Some Purpose* (Penguin), E. R. Emmett, *Learning to Philosophise* (Penguin), my own *Thinking with Concepts* (C.U.P.), and so forth.

to think rationally to learning a particular linguistic skill – to learning logic. People fail to think rationally, it is assumed, because they do not know how to: much as people might fail to measure distances and heights because they do not know enough geometry. But this is not what we see in practical living. We see, rather, men who can recognize illogicality, fallacies, or prejudice in other people, and who know perfectly well what it is to contradict oneself, draw a false conclusion, and so on, but who nevertheless just *are* illogical in some areas of their own thinking. It is not that they don't know *how to* think logically: it's rather that they just don't *do* it.

Our problem is of course why they don't, and what can be done to help them. But it is important to see first that this is so. Characteristically people often talk without thinking: we might say, without really meaning what they are saying. On these occasions, they are certainly 'using language' in a rather trivial sense: but one might just as well say that language is using them. Their words seem to have a life of their own: they are not meant, but just strung together carelessly. The words just *come out of them*, as it were, rather as words may come out of a parrot or a sleepwalker or a hypnotised person. They are not 'using language' in our broader sense at all.

It is not surprising that, when people behave like this, they speak illogically, commit fallacies, are deceived by propaganda and so forth. But this is not the cause of their behaviour: it is a symptom of it. The situation is not like that of a child who gets his sums wrong because he is ignorant of the multiplication tables: it is like that of a child who gets his sums wrong because he is not really trying, not attending, not thinking about the figures he is writing down. The proper remark to make of such cases is not 'Ah, you've committed a logical fallacy: you don't know about fallacies, so I'll explain . . .' but rather 'You don't really mean that, do you? Think about what you've just said, and see if you really think that those words do the job.'

In a way, we could describe the quality we are trying to produce here as a kind of truthfulness or honesty. A man may of course be untruthful or dishonest in a quite straightforward way, i.e. by telling a deliberate lie. He knows what is true and what is false, and says what is false. But there are also very many cases where men mislead themselves and other people without being so deliberate about it: rather, by a lack of deliberation which allows words to come from them that are only half-meant. Sometimes it is obvious that they are trying to deceive themselves as much as other people: trying for instance, to convince themselves that their prejudices are justified. All these are cases where people are behaving irrationally, not really thinking – due to prejudice, or fear, or some kind of desire or emotion: and their misuse of language is a symptom of this.

We may say, then, that misuse of language (committing fallacies, etc.) is not the prime cause of the trouble. It is not the misuse, but the *non*-use – the failure really to use conventional signs in an intentional and serious manner, as opposed to simply letting the signs flow from one unchecked. Essentially the same point can be made about human actions and non-linguistic behaviour. It rarely (if ever) happens that people deliberately act irrationally. What usually happens is that either they deliberate and act rationally, or else they just react – they are carried away by emotion, too apathetic to do more than drift and behave impulsively, and so forth.

Although it is possible to distinguish conceptually between motivation and ability in this area, it is often very hard to do in practice: and I do not propose to pursue the distinction at length here. The important thing is that men in general, and perhaps children and adolescents in particular, commonly lack the motivation and/or the ability. A great deal of research would be needed to be at all sure about the facts relevant here, particularly in the years of early childhood, which are plainly of great importance. What we have to do is to recognize this lack clearly, and hence to have some hope of devising teaching-methods which will overcome it.

It is easy enough to give a general description of what we are trying to teach here, and what the obstacles may be. Pupils may have all sorts of difficulties which prevent them from language-using; they may be in terror, under the influence of some inner compulsion, very stupid, lacking even the simplest vocabulary, and so forth. Some of these difficulties the teacher may not be able to overcome: some even a skilled psychiatrist may not be able to overcome. Much is of course due to the model which the pupil's parents, consciously or unconsciously, provide for him in the language-using area. But we can at least give them *practice :* we can try to inculcate the *habit* of language-using, as well as actually improving their performance in particular linguistic skills.

B. CONTEXT OF TEACHING

Of course we want to inculcate this habit in situations which the pupils meet in their everyday lives, rather than in a context of some particular discipline or subject which has no direct connection with morality or personal relationships. Much energy is expended by teachers on getting children to reflect rationally when they do mathematics or Latin: less – incredibly – is expended in more relevant contexts. Suitable topics for such reflection would include how a pupil behaves towards his friends: how he talks to his parents: his attitude to his teachers, and to others in a position of authority: his feelings about the opposite sex: his behaviour towards young people, and so forth. Such subject-matter as how he spends his pocket-money, what he does with his spare time, and how he likes to dress *may* be useful, but is likely to be less so than those topics mentioned above: for it is not clear that personal relationships are immediately involved.

But it is likely that the teacher or lecturer will not be able to rely on enough real-life situations arising within the institution. Even if such a situation does arise, we cannot be sure that it will arise in a *controlled context*: that is to say, a context in which we get the pupil to move from his natural behaviour into more and more reflective and sophisticated linguistic consideration of his behaviour. So the teacher will have to create such situations, either inside the institution or outside it. In nearly every school, however, it will be possible for most teachers to create the kind of situations needed. Going on an outing, deciding on school rules, putting on a play, giving a dance, building a swimming-pool, entertaining parents, doing some social work – these and many more are within the scope of all: and practising teachers do not need to be told by me what situations most suit their particular schools and pupils. We need only make the point that situations of this sort are required, and need to be invented. If this involves restructuring the life of the school, so much the better.[1]

We need to bring this language-teaching into real-life situations, just because they are real. But by the same token, it is very difficult to *use* such situations to the full for educational purposes. For example: suppose the pupils behave badly on a school outing, or when giving a dance. It is of no use waiting until the next day, and then getting up and giving them a moral lecture about it. Pointing irrationality out to people afterwards is unlikely to cut much ice. By then it is too late: they have perhaps forgotten (if indeed they ever realised) just what they did, and what came into their heads while they were doing it: they will have adopted certain attitudes and postures, particularly certain attitudes to a teacher or other

[1] See Part IV.

authority 'telling them off'. Everything has already happened: the situation is past, dead, and cannot be revived.

What then should we do? (1) One possibility is to use a context which can be *immediately repeated*: just as one might get a child to do another sum of the same kind, if he gets the first one wrong. If we tell the children something about what went wrong with the outing or the dance, and they have another outing or dance immediately afterwards, we should be more likely to achieve some results. But it would be much better (2) if we use some methods of *objectifying* the original situation. If, for instance, an external observer was taking notes about what the pupils said and did, or (better) if we had a tape-recording of this, or (better still) a film or video-tape recording, then we could confront the pupils with these objective accounts of what happened. *They could see and hear themselves behaving and talking.* In this way, and probably only in this way, could they learn to become more aware of themselves in such situations.

It is now apparent that what the teacher needs is a teaching-context which is *already* controlled, in the sense that he will find it easy to 'play back' the pupils' behaviour to the pupils themselves. The essence of the teacher's problem is how he can most effectively combine the two necessities (i) of using 'real' situations, and (ii) of using them in properly controlled contexts. This problem is not new: it is basically the same in all forms of education. (For instance, the teacher of French needs (i) to bring the children up against the practical need to speak French when in Paris, and also (ii) to use contexts in which they can learn to do this in a controlled and organized way. Making them find their way up the Eiffel Tower would achieve (i) but not (ii): making them learn French grammar for homework would achieve (ii) but not (i). Having a French boy in the class might combine both.)

These points imply that the teacher needs a *working group*, not just a class under instruction. They also suggest that the way in which this group is set up, its social organization, is likely to be at least as important as any specific teaching-*methods* which we might advocate. How many do we have in the group? How often do we use the group? Where does it meet? How do we keep the group together? Can we use existing forms or classes or groups? How would the groups fit into the school or college organization? And, above all, what does the group actually *do*? What functions or tasks does it have? These and similar questions will be considered in Part IV of this book. For the purposes of this Part I shall assume that the teacher has some context in which to operate – in the classroom, if nowhere else.

What we shall now do is to consider in detail *one* particular 'game' which seems of unusual importance. I shall now stop calling it a 'game', because it is a very serious business: it is, rather, a particular form of rule-governed activity or form of life. It is *one* form amongst many: and though for convenience I shall entitle it 'the discussion-form', it is important that the reader should be as clear as he can about the rules, limits and purpose of the form (in this respect the 'game' analogy may be helpful).

C. THE DISCUSSION-FORM

(i) DEFINITION

The communication-type which we shall be considering is a particular form of *discussion*. 'Discussion' is a loose term, bordering on argument or quarrelling on one side, and gossip on the other: we shall try to give it more precise boundaries.

1. First, the function or point of the discussion-form is that it should result in the best possible answer to various questions, which may be generalized in the form of 'What ought X to do?' or 'Is Y the case?': for instance, 'What should John do about his girl friend?', 'Should we have a school rule about swearing?', 'Are Mary's parents too strict with her?', 'Do old people like to live in the town or the country?', and so forth. The variety of questions is here infinitely wide. What defines the form is not so much the type of question, but rather that its function is to *answer questions* (rather than to gossip, let off steam, etc.), and that this function involves certain specific rules.

2. Secondly, the players or discussers have an equal status in the form. We are not here in an order-and-obedience context (as in the case of a ship's crew obeying the captain), or in a context where some one person has a special authority as an expert (as in the case of a class of children learning facts from a history teacher).

3. Thirdly, the 'success' of the answer to the question depends (in the definition of this form) not only on its actual merits as an answer, but on the degree to which it is accepted, and the reasons for it understood, by as many players as possible. This precludes both (a) reaching an answer which is popular and generally acceptable but which is in itself a bad answer, and (b) one person,

or a minority group, imposing an answer – or even a majority persuading the group to accept an answer by illegitimate methods, that is, methods that do not involve getting them to see the merits and reasons for the answer: for instance, by dressing up the answer in glamorous clothes, trying to make out that the answer will gain them credit with their friends or outside authorities, and so forth.

Of the many various discussion-forms that are in practice used, the case of a seminar in some respects approaches most nearly to the above conditions. Theoretically at least, seminar-type discussions involve players of equal status: nobody is supposed to use illegitimate methods of persuasion (mob-oratory, 'pulling rank', courting popularity, etc.): all players are trying to cooperate in a mutual effort to discover the truth. In the case of a committee we have the extra factor, also required by our form, of having to reach a *decision :* and provided that the committee-members are of equal status, and are not influenced by outside factors irrelevant to the problem under discussion, this example fits very well. In many committees, however, as in court-martials, some of the members have a higher rank, or status, than the others.

Some of this may seem very obvious: but it is important to distinguish this form from other forms or sets of forms: not least because this form is, in practice, very rarely used properly or in a 'pure' way. Most 'discussions' in real life are contaminated by other interests and objectives besides the objective of reaching the truth or answering a question about what to do. Two other functions in particular tend to break in on it:

1. The 'social reinforcement' or 'social-convention' function. In most social gatherings this dominates the discussion-function. Discussions of a sort are indeed held in pubs, tea-parties, family groups and so forth; but the aim of truth-finding usually takes second place to the (often tacit) conventions of such groups. Very often what looks like genuinely truth-seeking discussion is in fact no more than a highly ritualized set of statements and responses, in which the players go through the motions of discussing, but have no real intention to learn or to clarify. It is a form of gossip, which may sometimes sound like a discussion only because it is ostensibly about politics, or literature, or the latest film, but the subject might just as well be the football results, what the neighbours are doing, what happened during the war, what the newest

pop records are, or almost anything. For the subject is not important as a subject of discussion: the kind of talk that goes on about it is intended only to help people to communicate, to share, to feel that they are on the same network.

2. The 'letting off steam' or 'self-expressive' function. This function is served, informally, on those many occasions when individuals use a group-context to express their own feelings. Outbursts of temper, rejoicing, complaining, and many other expressions of emotion come under this heading. In a more formal way, the function is served by various 'psychotherapeutic' groups (T-groups, group dynamics, and so forth) where the members are encouraged and expected to show their feelings towards others in the group, as part of a 'cure' or treatment-system. Here again the distinction between this and the discussion-form is not one of subject, but of purpose. The subject of a discussion-form might well be the feelings of one individual towards another ('Does John feel jealous of James?', 'Why is Mary angry with her mother?'): but the function of the form is to discuss and reach the truth about these feelings, not to evoke them or encourage their direct expression. It would be in order, during a discussion-form, to say 'Yes, I do feel very angry with Roger', if the remark is relevant to the topic: but it would not be in order to say '— you, Roger, you — — ! !'

This will be sufficient to give the reader some idea of the definition of the form; in section (iii) we shall describe the rules in much more detail, so that the form may be more precisely defined.

(ii) USE
Why should we suppose that teaching children to use this form has any value? Remembering what we said in section A about the 'use of language', we may think of two general reasons:

1. First, and most obviously, people do often have to make up their minds about what to do, or what is the case, when they are in a group-situation (in a family, as gang-members, club-members, etc.); and the discussion-form simply *is* the right form for doing this. For (a) even if the decision affects only one individual, nevertheless that individual needs to ask help from those around him: he needs to be able to make his problems *public*, to accept advice and criticism, to face facts and doubts presented to him by others, and so forth. Further, (b) very often the decision involves the

whole group: and here it is essential that it be discussed – and so far as possible agreed – by all the members of the group, as equals, along the lines suggested above.

2. Secondly, there are powerful reasons for supposing that without experiences of this discussion-form the individual would never be able to think by himself and for himself at all. Of course it is true that there are some individuals who are good at thinking by themselves, and bad at using the discussion-form. Yet even these, if they really are good at thinking by themselves, must at some stage in their lives have learned what it is to think; and this, as we saw in Section A, means that they must have learned the use of a public language to solve problems. Almost certainly they will have learned something of this from their parents or friends in early childhood. But there are many children who have not learned this, or not learned it well: who have never had the experiences required to initiate them into this particular use of language and thought. This is why schools need to arrange for such initiation by instituting the discussion-form. It is not only thinking *in* a group, or thinking about the problems *of* a group, which is at stake: it is *any* kind of thinking.

The form, as defined by the rules we shall state in the next section, represents an ideal which may never be attained. This is common to all forms and games: nobody ever plays cricket or chess perfectly – indeed it is not clear what would be meant by saying such a thing. The merits of getting children to use the form are based on the modest assumption that conscious *understanding* and *practice* of the form according to the rules will help them to use it better, and induce them to use it more often when required in the outside world, i.e. not only at school. But there are two possible limitations on this:

1. Understanding and practice may be insufficient due to (a) lack of natural talent – a child may just not be *able* to keep some of the rules: (b) lack of motivation – a child may (consciously or unconsciously) not *want* to keep some of the rules.
2. Both ability and motivation may be present within the school situation, but not be transferred to situations outside the school.

These limitations are, of course, common to all forms of teaching and all educational arrangements. How serious they are is an open question. But there is some reason to believe that they are not serious enough to make us doubt the whole undertaking. We can, at least, develop the child's natural talents as far as possible by giving him understanding and practice in the form: and we can give him the *habit* of using it whenever it needs to be used, which in itself may help with the problem of motivation. Further, since the form can be very enjoyable, it should not be impossible for the imaginative teacher to solve the problem of motivation in other ways as well; and equally the problem of transferability may be tackled in ways which no doubt the teacher will be able to think of himself.

(iii) RULES AND ERRORS

It is worth our while to remember a threefold distinction in the rules of games between what I shall call 'constitutive' rules, 'penalized' rules, and 'rules of guidance'. The constitutive rules *define* the game: there are certain things which you are simply not allowed to do, like moving a castle diagonally in chess. If you do these things, the game stops: you have to make the move again, or start the game again. Penalized rules are rules which do not absolutely prevent you from doing things, but in virtue of which you are formally penalized for doing them: you *can* pick up the ball with your hands in association football, but then the referee blows his whistle and the other side gets a free kick. Rules of guidance do not involve either closing down the game, or any kind of formal penalty: they are just general principles which the player would be wise to follow, such as 'Never bring your queen out in the first few moves' in chess, or 'Always tackle low' in certain kinds of football, or 'Never trump your partner's ace' in bridge.

Now the discussion-form is not, in fact, an established game. In trying to establish it as something like a game – that is, as something which can be reasonably formalized, so that pupils can learn it more easily – we face the question of *how* formal to make it. This is the question of (a) how many constitutive rules to have – how many occasions there will be when the teacher formally closes down the game: and (b) how many penalized rules to have – how often to make the pupils pay some kind of formal penalty for breach of a rule; (c) the rules of guidance, will persist in any form: we want the pupils to discuss (play) well, and there is no *a priori* limit on the number of guiding principles we can give them.

For our particular purpose here, I shall say that (a) the only constitutive rules shall be (1) that the medium of the form is *talk* or *words*: that is, the form should only be closed down (and perhaps restarted soon afterwards) if the pupils do something like throw things at each other or attack each other physically, or stop talking altogether; (2) that there shall be a general intention on the part of the pupils to talk *in this mode*, i.e. to discuss with the object of 'finding the answer' as described in section (i) above, and some success in doing so. I shall say further that (b) and (c) can be merged, abolishing (b): that is, there shall be no formal penalties. Note will be taken of pupils doing particularly badly, and they may be reminded, rebuked, or discouraged in various ways by the teacher as he sees fit, but there are to be no rules with specified sanctions attached, as there are in many games.

The point of spelling this out is that we are here considering only *one* form, or more precisely only *one version* of the discussion-form. It would be desirable that teachers should try other versions, for which the arrangements I have specified in the above paragraph might not be the best. Thus, it would be possible to make the pupils use a more formal version, in which category (b) appeared. For instance, suppose we gave each pupil twenty points and then deducted points for certain kinds of errors (e.g. if he raises his voice above a certain pitch, a buzzer is sounded and he loses a point: if he is wildly irrelevant he loses two points: if he shows hostility he loses three points, and so on). We should thus introduce the notion of *winning* the game, which in our version is absent: in our version, the group functions more or less well in the discussion, and individual incompetence is noticed only informally.

Our form is, in fact, pretty informal throughout. But we must not make it too informal. We can specify to the pupils the (very simple) constitutive rules mentioned above, (1) that the medium shall be talk, and (2) that they shall try to use *this* form and not some other. The defining principles under (2) – what *makes* it 'this form' – should of course be explained at length to the children, with examples, before starting: though they will also learn the nature of the form as they play, by having their errors pointed out. Here the teacher has much latitude. If (2) is only minimally satisfied, in that the children do in a sense try to discuss but nevertheless spend most of the time (say) insulting each other or gossiping, then the teacher can say 'Look, it seems that we are not using this form (playing this game) any more, I shall close it down and start again.'

Apart from this, we can only list items in category (c), the rules of guidance. It is best to do this negatively, i.e. by a brief description of the sorts of errors or 'bad play' that can be made. I here distinguish between (I) wrong attitude or role, and (II) wrong moves or style: but it will be clear that items in I may be responsible for items in II (e.g. 'hostility' will generate 'speaking too loudly').

I. WRONG ATTITUDE OR WRONG ROLE
  1. Being irrelevantly influenced by personal considerations, e.g. the status or role of another participant (a teacher, a younger or 'inferior' pupil, etc.); his manners, accent, dress, facial appearance, or bodily posture; particular relationship to oneself (friend, enemy, brother, etc.); or his style of speaking (weighty, vehement, amusing, etc.).
  2. Being over-emotional about the subject (over-earnest).
  3. Lacking sufficient animus about the subject (too dry, bored, etc.).
  4. Being hostile or aggressive.
  5. Showing off, playing a 'clown-role'.
  6. Over-placating, being subservient.
  7. Wanting to be 'social' rather than 'find the answer' (using the group for social reinforcement rather than as a task-performing group).
  8. Being obstinate, too retentive of one's own opinion.
  9. Being negative (not wanting the group to make progress).
  10. Being jealous of others' contributions.

II. WRONG MOVES OR WRONG STYLE
  1. Interrupting others.
  2. Under-contributing (length of each contribution too short or numbers of contributions too few).
  3. Over-contributing (length too great or numbers too great).
  4. Speaking too loudly.
  5. Speaking too softly.
  6. Speaking too quickly.
  7. Speaking too slowly.
  8. Not ensuring that one has understood (e.g. by asking the other to repeat or clarify).
  9. Not really listening to the other.
  10. Not replying to what the last person has said.
  11. 'Blocking' (e.g. saying 'This is all pretty silly', 'I don't see the point of all this', etc.). (See I.9 above.)
  12. Not *showing* that one has taken the other's point.
  13. Making remarks *ad hominem* ('Well, *you* don't always do what you say we should', 'You're a fine one to talk!', etc.).

14. Bringing in irrelevant cases ('I once knew a man who . . .', 'My Aunt Doris . . .').
15. Over-stating ('There's absolutely no doubt that . . .', 'Any intelligent person will agree that . . .').
16. Not 'oiling the wheels' (e.g. just saying 'No', rather than 'Sorry, I don't quite see why you say that . . .').
17. Pretending to undue clarity (instead of saying, e.g. 'I'm not quite sure how to put this, but I feel something like such-and-such, can anyone help me with what I'm trying to say . . .?').
18. Not noticing the importance of word-meanings.
19. Not recognizing straightforward factual issues, about which one can defer to an expert, or which one can look up in a book.
20. Miscellaneous types of irrelevance.

These lists are to some extent arbitrary, in that they are not exhaustive (I have given a round number of 10 in I and 20 in II), and in that the items may overlap. I do not think it would be worth while trying to specify these errors, and their overlaps and sub-types, more exactly here: it will be better for the teacher to make his own observations and form his own categories. It is important, though, that he should do this, rather than be content merely to say or think things like 'The discussion isn't keeping to the point', or 'Aren't we getting a bit heated?' We must have *some* list of identifiable errors if we are to make it easier for the pupils to learn how to use the form properly.

(iv) TEACHING THE FORM

Here too it will be best simply to list a number of things which the teacher may find helpful:

1. Explain the nature of the form carefully, with much preliminary discussion, and distinguish it from other forms (e.g. gossip, social reinforcement, expression of emotion, etc.) by the use of examples.
2. Put up the rules (both the constitutive rules and the rules of guidance) on the blackboard, so that they can be visible throughout, and referred to when necessary.
3. Sound a bell or buzzer (or make some other formalized sign), as often as he thinks fit, when a rule of guidance has been infringed.
4. Try out various methods of formalizing the discussion, e.g.: (a) collect general 'ideas' or opinions first, and put them on the

blackboard anonymously: when that stage is over, get the ideas and opinions themselves discussed one by one.

(b) call for each pupil's opinion in turn.

(c) get the pupils, or groups of pupils, to write down their opinions and read them out.

(d) persuade the pupils to collect evidence in the first stage: then consider the evidence with a view to coming to a decision.

(e) giving regular breaks for thinking, during which talking is forbidden.

(These are just a few of the possible methods.)

5. Experiment with the immediate social context or 'staging' of the discussion. (Does it work best if the pupils are behind desks? Sitting in a circle? In comfortable or uncomfortable chairs? On the floor? Should there be no adults, or more than one adult? Does it help if they have food and/or drink provided while discussing? Is it better if the discussions take place in a classroom, or in an informal setting? And so on.)

6. Use all possible methods of objectifying the discussion (tape-recordings or video-tape played back to the pupils afterwards: outside observers commenting on the discussion: the pupils attending discussions by other groups).

7. Discuss the discussion itself, either immediately afterwards or after the tape-recording has been heard; perhaps then repeating the original discussion on the same subject to see if they can do better, talk less irrelevantly, etc.

8. Move from simple, practical discussion-questions ('How can we help the weaker members of the class to improve their work?') to more general questions ('What should be the basis of the school rules?').

9. Moving from topics in which emotion is already invested ('Do you like your teacher?') to more neutral topics ('Should the police arrest demonstrators?') or experience may show it to be necessary to move in the opposite way, because some topics may be too 'emotional' and hence threatening.

10. Make it quite clear to the children that it is their honest opinion, sensibly given, which is required, that they should forget about friends, authorities and other irrelevancies, and simply concentrate on finding the right answer. This involves making the role of the teacher as referee only, for this particular form, as clear as possible.

(v) TRAINING FOR THE FORM
Another non-exhaustive list:

1. Encouraging fluency by getting pupils to talk about almost anything.
2. Asking pupils to criticise discussions, e.g. on TV programmes or played to them on a tape-recorder.
3. Debates, mock trials, and other more formal contexts which encourage language-use.
4. Making the pupils talk without any preparation.
5. Making them describe or advocate something within a limited time (e.g. 'Say *in 30 seconds* why you think so-and-so', two-minute speeches, etc.).
6. Training in 'social skills' of the kind necessary for the game (e.g. training in basic social rituals such as apologizing, pointing out errors, thanking, praising, asking for clarification, etc.): and in non-linguistic social skills (non-verbal communication).
7. Making the pupils talk under *any* conditions (with a noise going on, to younger/older people, at a party standing up, sitting in an armchair, addressing the whole school, etc.).
8. Making them unafraid to express unpopular opinions (e.g. which their friends will disagree with, or which they may think unacceptable to the staff).
9. Making them use other forms, so that they may contrast the discussion-form with the others.
10. Giving practice in accelerating or decelerating the speed of their talk.

Perhaps I shall already have incurred the boredom of the imaginative teacher, who is perfectly capable of listing these rules and hints for himself. But I would impress on the reader that it is easy to say, in a vague and general way, 'Pupils ought to learn how to discuss sensibly', but hard to formalize the principles and methods that will make such learning coherent. My advice would be 'If you can make a better list, excellent: but for goodness' sake do *formalize*, don't be vague, give the pupils something to measure up to, a clear account of how to use this form well, so that they know where they are and you know where you are.' For this form, or 'game', as I have called it earlier, is too serious and too important for the development of rationality in general (not just morality) to be left in a muddle.

PART III

Rules and Contracts

In our first publication[1] we tried to show that the morally educated person is not one who merely obeys, or conforms to, a particular authority or set of rules. We there described such a person as *rational* and *autonomous*: that is, roughly, able to make up his own mind sensibly and reasonably about what is right and wrong. But this does not at all mean that moral education has nothing to do with rules, obedience, contracts and authority. On the contrary: adherence to rules and contracts is demanded by concern for other people's interests (PHIL). It is an essential part of moral education to develop this concern, to increase pupil's awareness of how failure in this area affects other people's feelings (EMP) and the general social situation (GIG), and to motivate the pupil so that he can live up to this concern and awareness (KRAT). This, then, is an area in which all the 'moral components' are required, and by means of which all of them may be developed.

We shall begin by trying to get clear about just what attitude towards this area of rules and contracts we want to encourage in the pupil: what sort of understanding of it we want him to develop. Unless we are ourselves clear, it is not likely that any of the practical methods we shall go on to outline will be effective. We must have a sure grasp what is *rational* or *reasonable* in this area. This is not easy, because we ourselves, as well as our pupils, tend often to misunderstand the area and lapse into postures that may be labelled 'authoritarian', 'liberal', 'progressive', 'Victorian', etc. – all of which postures are partly the result of mere muddle and prejudice.

A. Rules and Frameworks

Rules and authorities in a school, or any other institution, or in society generally, are not to be regarded as ends in themselves. They

[1] *I.M.E.*, Chapter 2.

are not there by divine right, so to speak, or because the authorities are powerful and can make people obey. For it must always be possible to question the rules or the authorities, to think about whether they are right or wrong. To put it another way: getting people to think, to make up their own minds reasonably, comes first, and the function of rules and authorities must be subordinated to this end.

Very roughly, this is the underlying assumption of a liberal society as opposed to a totalitarian or dictatorial one. People sometimes think that a liberal society means one in which you can do as you like, whereas in a totalitarian society you do what you are told. But, in fact, all societies have rules and authorities: the real difference is in what the function of the rules and authorities is supposed to be. In liberal societies the function is to give people freedom and security so that they can think for themselves: in totalitarian ones the rules and authorities make up the individual's mind for him – he is not supposed to think or question, but just to obey the rules or be indoctrinated into whatever the authorities think is best for him (or for them). What we object to in totalitarian societies, like Nazi Germany, is not just that they had bad rules and bad authorities: much more important is that they felt they had the right to tell people what to think. They used rules and authorities to produce the sort of people with the sort of beliefs they wanted.

But once we understand this, another thing becomes obvious: and that is, that what rules and authorities you have is just as important for liberal societies as for totalitarian ones. You cannot help people to think, or educate them, or bring them up to be free and reasonable, just by leaving them alone and having no rules at all. People sometimes talk as if anything you could call a 'rule' must somehow be a wicked thing imposed by some tyrannical authority. But in fact without following rules we would not be human beings at all. Rules are needed to play games, do business, drive cars, arrange for people to be fed and housed, and for every other human activity. What distinguishes human beings from animals is that human beings are rule-following creatures. You cannot think or talk without following rules, the rules of language. A child who was never taught the rules of language would not grow up to be human.

Every child, and every adult too, needs a framework and a set of rules. It is not just that he feels more secure in such a framework, though (particularly for young children) that is also true: it is rather that, without such a framework, he will never learn anything. For instance, if we want to teach something to two children in a primary school, we cannot even begin to do this if they are fighting, or not listening, or drunk, or suffering terribly from toothache. We have to arrange for certain *preconditions* for educating people to be established: in particular, we have to arrange things so that they can communicate with each other and learn from other people.

This is very much like the rules needed to make the methods of even the most liberal society work at all. A primitive society might settle its disputes by fighting, so that the strongest party wins: then perhaps we make progress, and agree to talk things over by means of a discussion or a parliamentary debate. But this at once means that we have to have rules: you cannot have a discussion or a debate if people are throwing spears at each other. Indeed the rules you need to follow in order to get a good discussion or debate are quite complicated: it does not work well if people insult or shout at each other, or just hurl abuse, or keep interrupting. You need rules of procedure. You also, of course, have to make sure that people are not too ill or upset to discuss things: that they are adequately defended against their external enemies: that they have had enough to eat, and so forth.

We have to remember, then, that rules are supposed to have a point or purpose – to make a better game, to get a proper discussion, or whatever. Of course some rules may not have much point, and can be scrapped: other rules may be very important and well-suited to what we are trying to do: others again may need some improvement or additions. It all depends on what we are out to achieve. We have to have one kind of rule for a company of soldiers in battle, another for a cricket team, and another for a classroom discussion or a parliamentary debate. None of these have to be 'moral' rules, if by that is meant that we look on them as ideally right or good in themselves. It is just that they serve particular human needs or wants or interests.

This is why both the notion of total conformity and the notion of total anarchy are logically absurd for human beings. For (1) if people always obeyed the rules, never questioning them but simply going through the patterns of behaviour which the rules prescribed, we would not be able to distinguish them from animals governed entirely by their instincts – like birds building nests, or ants or bees. It is part of the concept of a human being that he is capable of not conforming – that if he follows rules, then to some extent he does so deliberately and of his own free will. But equally (2), and for similar reasons, anarchy is impossible for human beings. For to be human means, at least, that one learns to talk and think by conforming to the rules governing language and meaning: and apart from this basic consideration, anything which we could properly call a society would involve a number of human beings making some kind of contracts with each other – and contracts are a form of rule-keeping. Those who call themselves 'anarchists' are usually protesting (whether they know it or not) against *particular* authorities or *particular* kinds of rules, not against having any rules at all.

All this means that what sort of rules we ought to have, in particular contexts and for particular purposes, is a very open question, which can often only be settled by finding out more facts than we know already. For instance, it is pretty obvious that for many (perhaps all) purposes, we need to have rules about telling the truth, keeping promises, and not hurting or killing people. It would be hard to see how any communal activity could flourish if we did not, for the most part, abide by such rules: though of course we may make exceptions in special cases. But there will be plenty of other cases where we are not sure whether we need rules in a certain area or not, or are not sure about what actual rules to have.

For example, we might agree that for the purposes of having an efficient army we had to subject the soldiers to certain disciplinary regulations. Obviously one rule must be that they obey their officers. But what about making them keep their uniforms clean, and drill on the parade ground? Some would argue that this is a waste of time, and that their efficiency as a fighting force would not be impaired – or might even be improved – if there were no rules in this area. Others might claim that cleanliness of uniform and drill contributed to efficiency. In fact, of course, we cannot be sure of the answer to this: we might have to rely on guesswork and the collective experience of army officers. But we would try to settle the question, not by saying (1) that soldiers *just ought* to conform to these rules, nor by saying (2) that the rules were just silly traditions or conventions which ought to be scrapped at once. We would settle the question on the evidence, and try to find out whether or not such rules contributed to the purposes which we wished to achieve.

Again, we might agree that at a university or college the purpose of having students there was so that they might learn certain subjects efficiently. So it would obviously be necessary to have rules of some kind or other which ensured that they worked reasonably hard, read the right books, turned up for lectures, or whatever was thought essential to the purpose of learning. But what about rules governing their 'private lives' – for instance, rules about sexual behaviour or dress? Here too we must not be doctrinaire: we must not say, with unthinking conformity, that they just ought to keep certain rules because this produces 'decent behaviour' or 'proper manners'; but nor must we say, with an over-hasty rebelliousness, that the rules are certainly irrelevant to the purpose. It might be the case that certain types of sexual behaviour affect the student's ability to learn – for good or ill: or it might be the case that they make no difference.

B. CONTRACTS AND DECISION-PROCEDURES

(i) THE CONCEPT OF CONTRACT

Young children are not, in general, capable of making up their own rules in a sensible way: indeed, they are not capable of understanding the kind of considerations mentioned above. They would not be able to understand them, unless we made them follow certain rules in the first place: for only so could they come to grasp the whole idea of rules and the purpose of rules. So in effect parents and teachers *initiate* children into certain contexts which are governed by rules, in the hope that when they are older and have learnt more about the world they will be able to make up their own minds in a reasonable way. We give children more and more freedom as they get older, until when they are adult we allow them to choose their own way of life for themselves.

Naturally there are difficulties about the particular point at which it seems right to consider children as 'grown up'. But in general, we feel that we have some kind of mandate or right to supervise young children: we do not regard them as completely free and responsible agents, so we curtail their liberty; and in return we look after them – feed, house, clothe and protect them, give them education and guidance, and so forth. At some time – perhaps at the school-leaving age, when they can be economically independent if they wish – we give up this mandate. Thereafter we hope that they may wish to continue being educated, and will want to learn from other people in our society: but we cannot enforce this. This is the position that applies, in some degree at least, to sixth-formers, university and college students, and so forth.

But when the child or adolescent is considered to be adult, and has become free of the particular rules which parents and teachers imposed upon him, he does not thereby become free of all rules. It is in principle possible that he may be able to live entirely by himself on a desert island, owing nothing to and being owed nothing by any other person: but even this is in practice impossible (all desert islands belong to somebody nowadays). In fact he will go to college, or do a job, or at any rate exist as a member of some sovereign state – Great Britain, or France, or somewhere else. Unlike the young child, he can opt for one out of a number of possibilities: he does not *have* to go to college, if he dislikes Britain he can emigrate, and so on. But he will certainly find himself within some rule-governed situation or other.

This means that, in effect, he enters more or less consciously and deliberately into some kind of *contract*. This may not be an obvious and ordinary contract, such as that between a worker and an employer, or one business man and another: but it will be a contract just the same. It is helpful here to think of choosing a contract in the light of choosing whether to play a particular game. By choosing to play cricket, or bridge, or anything else, one contracts to obey a particular set of rules in common with other people. Often the rules do not cover every possible contingency, so that there are authorities empowered to interpret them, like umpires in cricket and referees in football: and part of the contract is that the players are supposed to accept the umpire's or referee's ruling – he is, so to speak, part of the rules of the game. In just the same way, in any society, there will be rules (sometimes in the form of constitutions) and authorities: chairmen, parliaments, vice-chancellors, headmasters, school committees and so forth.

Of course these contracts work both ways: the contractor not only is obliged to obey the rules, but also is entitled to receive benefits under the rules. For instance, part of the contract in this country is that citizens pay income tax, the money from which is spent on things like roads, education, a health service and so on, which are of use to those citizens. At a university, students agree to obey the rules about lectures, reading books, etc. and receive in return the teaching and opportunities for learning which the university provides. In the army, soldiers accept military law, in return for which the army clothes, feeds and in general looks after the soldiers.

However, as we have seen, rules and contracts which embody rules can be changed. In order to make a change, we need some kind of *decision-procedure*; that is, some kind of agreement about legitimate and illegitimate ways of changing the rules. Thus if we were forming a social club, or a small society on a desert island, we should probably think something like this: Well, let's have such-and-such rules for the time being, since these seem the most sensible ones: but maybe we shall want to change them in the future. Now what shall we do – shall we elect a boss who can change the rules when he wants, or a small committee of three people who can change them? Or shall we say that everybody must vote, and that the rules can only be changed if there is a majority of more than 50 per cent? Or should we require a two-thirds majority? Or what?' In coming thus to agree about what ways of changing the rules we *were* going to allow, we should also be agreeing about what ways we were *not* going to allow. For instance, we should probably say 'We'll discuss changes in the rules, but people mustn't keep shouting or fighting during the discussions. We will allow people to make speeches, or carry banners with slogans, but we won't allow them to throw bricks or spears', and so forth.

So here we have, not just the ordinary rules, but rules-about-changing-rules, rules about decision-procedures. In any large society this usually means some agreement about the 'sovereign body', the ultimate court of appeal: in this country Parliament is normally taken to be sovereign, but in other countries it might be a particular oligarchy, or a dictator, or the will of the people as expressed in a vote or referendum. And there will also be rules, more or less clearly stated, about what is allowable by way of trying to change the rules: putting pressure on a Member of Parliament, or peaceful demonstration, or speaking in Hyde Park, are all legitimate; throwing bombs or assassinating Prime Ministers are not.

All this is going to apply to any society, any contractual situation or 'game' played in common: even to a small society of two members, as with a married couple. We may hope, of course, that it may not be necessary to spell out all the rules all the time: in marriage, for instance, the couple may get on together so well that they need not bother to keep thinking about their contractual obligations or decision-procedures. But on the other hand, if there is any trouble or difficulty, we are inevitably thrown back on some such agreement. The only alternative to such agreement is for a person to opt out of that particular society altogether.

It is not likely that we shall be able to offer every individual exactly the sort of 'game' or contract which he likes. I might prefer to have the rules of cricket changed, so that I am not obliged to spend long and boring hours fielding rather than batting: but if I cannot get them changed, then either I must play cricket and put up with having to field, or else I cannot play cricket. Similarly, in any contract or society, there will probably be things which I dislike, or of which I morally disapprove, or which I regard as irrational, tiresome, silly, scandalous or wicked. Naturally I will try to get these changed but if I want to join the society at all, then (1) I am obliged to keep the rules in the meantime, and (2) I am obliged to restrict myself to allowable methods of getting the rules changed, since the rules about what methods are allowable are themselves amongst the rules I contract for.

Thus if you are born and brought up in England, you are faced with a choice. By remaining part of the system, you get whatever advantages the system has – such things as a health service, social security if you are out of work, free education, law and order, and so forth. You have the right to try to change any rules you disapprove of by certain methods. On the other hand, you have to keep the rules which permit these advantages – paying income tax, not stealing, etc. – and the rules which disallow certain methods of change, such as using violence on other people or setting fire to buildings. Thus you are not obliged to believe that all the rules are particularly good rules, or that the values enshrined in English society are the right ones: but you are obliged to play the game according to the rules. You can either accept this contractual obligation if you think it is worth your while, or else you can refuse and emigrate.

All this would remain true in any situation or society. But this is not to say that the rules we have in any society are good ones. In particular, we may think that the rules about decision-procedures, and the general structure of many societies, are very unsatisfactory in that they do not allow enough people to participate in making decisions enough of the time. Situations develop in which society gets divided into 'we', who are on the receiving end of the rules, and 'they' who make the rules. Workers, students and others feel that the rules are not *their* rules. Of course, even if they are not, they still have to decide whether to contract for them or to opt out of society altogether: but it is quite understandable that they feel left out of the most important part of the game, that is, left out of making up and changing the rules. There is a lot to be said about how to make societies more democratic, bring more people into the game, and hence avoid these difficulties, and it is very important that particular societies – not only countries like England, but also smaller societies like universities and schools – should devote a good deal of thought to this.

When such difficulties arise, a good deal of trouble is caused by *lack of clarity about the contract*. For instance, to take a topical case, the university authorities may have a very vaguely-stated expectation that the students will 'behave reasonably' or 'not bring the university into disrepute'. But this might be interpreted quite differently, in practice, by the authorities and the students. If what was meant by 'behaving reasonably' were clearly spelled out, and the students asked either to contract for this or else not to come to the university, we could avoid trouble. So too with other situations; trouble arises partly because it is just *not clear what the rules are*. If everyone shares common values and ways of behaving, this doesn't matter much: but we live in a time when this is not true, and the only thing is to get both parties to state clearly what rules they want to contract for.

This is something which students, workers and others who often feel that rules are just authoritarian impositions can try to achieve. Too often we see authorities trying simply to maintain their authority without clarity about rules and without clear justifications of the rules, and those under the authority's control simply rebelling in an aimless aggressive way, dissatisfied with the system but without any clear views about what changes are required. There are vested interests on both sides: the authorities may mask theirs by talking about 'law and order', 'decent behaviour' and so forth; and the underdogs may deceive themselves that they are acting out of idealism, reformist zeal, etc.

This applies, of course, not only to the contracts in society (e.g. the U.K.) or in institutions (e.g. a university), but also to contracts in particular social contexts. To take a topical example: if somebody comes to speak at a meeting, he will want to know what the rules of the meeting are to be. Here there are various possibilities: one may have rules which allow heckling, as seems to be the case in some political assemblies, or rules which allow demonstrations making it impossible for the speaker to speak, or rules which allow throwing eggs (in which case the speaker may bring eggs of his own), or almost anything. What matters is that the rules are specified before-hand, and enforced. Again, either we can have a football match in which the players just play football without interference: or we can allow a situation in which police, casual spectators, demonstrators and others prevent any football being played at all: or, if we really want it, I suppose we can have a sort of mob scene in which football may be played (if the police win) or may not (if the demonstrators win). Any of these rule-governed systems or 'games' may be specified in advance.

Naturally various people will have a vested interest in *not* having the rules clearly specified. These may be the authorities, who keep the rules deliberately vague in order (perhaps) to be able to clamp down on any particular piece of behaviour which in their opinion, or 'public opinion', or the opinions of a certain social class, is distasteful or disruptive. (Law and law-enforcement about obscenity, censorship, and sexual matters generally seem to be of this kind.) Or they may be minority groups who wish to take advantage of unclear rule-systems in order to make their will felt. Anyone who has ever found himself in an authority-role will readily appreciate the temptation to leave things unspecified, to 'smudge it', 'let sleeping dogs lie', etc.: and anyone who has ever found himself in a minority group which feels passionately about some cause or other will readily understand how such groups may benefit from lack of contractual clarity. But it will not do. Some contractual system must be logically and morally prior to any particular moves we may make to advance particular causes or beliefs.

This is not to say, of course, that it is desirable (or even possible) for us to formulate in advance rules to cover *every* contingency. We may well think it better, in many cases, to empower some authority to decide *ad hoc* on what is permissible and what is not: and in any case we shall need an authority (judge, umpire, etc.) to interpret the rules. But this too can be made absolutely clear. Thus, if I know that there are *some* clear rules governing my behaviour as a teacher, but that otherwise my behaviour will be accepted or objected to, rewarded or punished, at the discretion of the headmaster, then at least I know where I am: I can study the headmaster and act accordingly. Again, if we want a set-up in which the police can punish behaviour in the area of sex and obscenity more or less at will, or under cover of extremely vague laws, then (regrettable though this may be) at least we must be honest and proclaim that this *is* the set up. How much latitude should be given to authorities is a question that can only be answered by considering each case on its own merits: what is important is that the answer in each case should be clearly specified.

(ii) MORAL CONSENSUS

It will be worth our while here to take a look at some common but misguided alternatives to the contract system. They can for our purposes be lumped together, because they all attempt to substitute some first-order consensus for the second-order principle of contractual agreement. This first-order consensus is not often spelled out in detail, in the form of specific moral judgements about precisely what clothes should be worn, what exact types of sexual behaviour are good and bad, etc.: more commonly reference is made to what is 'reasonable', what 'most right-minded people would accept', 'decent behaviour', and so forth. In one form or another, this is perhaps the most popular approach in almost all societies to specific problems of misconduct. It is a kind of modern-dress version of saying 'It's just not *done*', with the implication that no 'right-minded' ('decent', 'reasonable', etc.) person would do it.

So long as such a consensus actually exists widely and strongly enough, then of course sufficient uniformity of behaviour and social expectations can be achieved. But it hardly needs pointing out that, in most industrialized societies today, it does not exist: if it did, the problems that we are trying to cope with would not exist either. So long, for instance, as Oxbridge or other students shared a common intuitive perception about what counted as 'gentlemanly behaviour', or what could be said to 'bring the university into disrepute', and so long as this intuitive perception carried enough weight for them to determine their conduct by it, then there simply could not *be* demonstrations, slogans painted on college walls, or cricket pitches destroyed in the name of racial integration. So long as sixth formers and other adolescents accepted the code of behaviour expected of them by teachers and other adults, they were part of the consensus and would not (almost by definition) act against it.

This sort of consensus does not have to be spelled out in detail, because it relies on the acceptance of a kind of authority. Certain people – parents, teachers, dons, or 'public opinion' as evidenced by friends and neighbours – are regarded as the touchstones or arbiters for determining the content of the consensus in each case. Thus a schoolboy or student who was uncertain about whether it was 'acceptable' or 'decent' not to wear a tie on some occasion, or to kiss his girl friend in public, would try to settle the question by asking himself what his schoolteacher or tutor would think about it. The breakdown in the consensus in our times has been dramatic precisely because these authorities or arbiters are no longer accepted as such by many people: it is not so much that such people disagree about this or that specific application of the consensus, but rather that the whole consensus has fallen into disregard because the adults who back it and instantiate it have fallen into disregard as authorities. When this happens, the game is wide open, for the defining rules are no longer accepted: it is not a question of replacing one rule within the game by another preferred rule, but rather of rejecting the whole game.

It is fatal (and fatally common) either to pretend that the consensus exists when it does not, or to attempt a new consensus of the same kind. This is a classic error committed by nearly all those in some position of authority, whether as governments, vice-chancellors, headmasters or whatever. What happens is something like this. First, the authorities will pretend or even believe that there is no problem: 'really' the consensus still exists – it is just a few unruly students or drunken rioters who cause the trouble: the majority of right-thinking citizens still have a clear idea of what is good and bad. Then, if trouble nevertheless persists, the authorities will make certain fashionable concessions: perhaps they now allow demonstrations in the streets provided they are not *too* violent, or they let students stay out till 2 a.m. instead of just till 10 p.m., or they no longer insist that sixth formers wear school uniform. By such measures they seem to themselves to be 'modern', 'progressive', 'in keeping with the times', etc., and avoid the image of Victorian sternness. Nowadays we are all to some degree 'permissive'.

What is boring and dangerous about this is that it fails to meet the problem at all. *Ad hoc* measures of this sort represent nothing more than a vague desire to be fashionable, and a hand-to-mouth attempt to keep trouble down to a minimum – to keep the students and adolescents, the trades unionists and negroes, the potential trouble-makers of whatever kind, *in play*, and to avoid an explosion. The implication is that the authorities are still posing as parents, and pretending that they are acknowledged as such by their citizens. How 'authoritarian' or 'liberal', 'Victorian' or 'progressive', 'tough-minded' or 'permissive' they are is, in fact, not to the point at all: this dimension is in no way relevant to our problem. For the problem here is not just what sort of rules there should be, but how to get a proper contractual basis for whatever sort of rules there are.

(iii) ACCEPTANCE AND RESTITUTION

A proper understanding of rules and contracts will issue in something which is of overwhelming importance for this whole area – something which education in this area is primarily out to generate: the *sincere acceptance* of certain contracts. This connects, both in theory and in practice, with other notions. If I sincerely accept a contract, and acknowledge the morally binding force of the rules it involves, it does not follow that I shall always keep the rules: but it does follow that I shall *repent* of my breach of the contract, *acknowledge* my error, and be willing to make some kind of *restitution* for the damage done.

It is worth noticing that these elements are commonly, and horrifically, absent in many practical situations. This may be largely due to the failure of educators and authorities to present pupils and citizens with a clearly-defined and detailed contract, so that (one might say) they have no chance to make any such sincere acceptance – indeed, not much chance of grasping the concept of a contract at all. I am not anxious to apportion blame, and we shall pursue practical suggestions to remedy the situation later: but it exists. It is simply not the case that juvenile delinquents, rioters, law-breakers and pupils at school who contravene the rules have sincerely accepted the laws and rules that they transgress. The point emerges in the disparity between what a person may feel himself expected to say, and what he really thinks. One delinquent convicted of stealing said to the magistrate in court 'Yeah, well, I'm sorry, I got carried away, I know it's wrong. I won't do it again': interviewed later, he said 'I didn't make the ——ing rules. Some people have too much money anyway: I needed a new bike', and so forth.

A large number not only of criminals but of ordinary students and pupils are in what can only be described as a state of war in society. Not necessarily *against* society: not all of them feel that the 'they' who make the rules are trying to do down the 'we' who have to keep them: though such persecutory feelings are apt to be easily generated, and may be commonly found. But many people are, if not hostile to society, at least *disconnected* from it: the 'they' may not be regarded as tyrants, but are still dissociated from the 'we'. 'We' are the students, young people, 'the gang', the comparatively poor, the Catholics, the negroes, the drop-outs: 'we' do not necessarily hate society, but 'we' are indifferent to it and do not regard ourselves as contractually bound by its laws. Some of 'us' may want to fight a 'hot war' with society, others a 'cold war'; others again merely profess total indifference.

We are accustomed to the difficulties of re-educating such people: we do not expect a high recovery rate from Borstals or prisons; the tender-minded of us regard them as mental cases whom it is not easy to cure, the tough-minded as hardened crooks or villains. But it is important to be clear what sort of situation we are dealing with, what sort of difficulties we have to overcome. It is *not*, in many cases, that such people lapse (however frequently) from a contract and set of rules which they acknowledge and accept. They do *not* think, in general and in their saner moments, that what they do is wrong. They may call it 'wrong' in inverted commas, meaning merely that it is liable to be punished, that 'society' or 'they' (the authorities) think it wrong, etc. But they do not think it wrong in the essential prescriptive sense of the word: that is, they have not *chosen* or *committed* themselves to trying to adjust their actual behaviour.

Because of this, the essential element in any kind of cure or re-education is often missing. Quite simply, such people do not want to be cured or re-educated: they prefer a situation in which they can carry on doing what they want, even if they sometimes get punished for it. They have formed their own norms and principles quite independently of any social contract or set of agreements. If the authorities are firm enough (as they should be), they may be more effectively deterred from behaving in certain ways: but this does nothing to change their basic attitude. Moreover, as respect for the established authorities and for any 'moral consensus' falls away, the strength of such deterrents has to increase in order to compensate for the loss of other motivation: and it is doubtful whether even such increased deterrents can be made strong, practical and effective enough to do the job. It is more sensible to tackle the problem in the educational field: and this means getting the sincere acceptance of contracts that we need.

(iv) 'AUTHORITY'
The current and fashionable distaste for what are vaguely described as 'authoritarian' procedures in education masks a number of important distinctions, which are important for children to grasp and which can only be grasped in the context of the games-and-contract approach. Here again our practice will be incompetent unless *we* first grasp the distinctions firmly.

Briefly, there are two kinds of 'authority' about which we should have no worries:

1. The 'authority' which a person has in a group, resulting from agreement or acceptance by the group of certain delegated and legitimized powers. An elected leader, the accepted captain of a games team, etc., are examples.

2. The 'authority' which a person has by virtue of superior knowledge in a particular area: thus A may be an authority on Polish history, B an authority on vintage cars, etc.

In both these cases there are good reasons why the authorities should be listened to and obeyed, to the extent that is covered by their authority. And it is important for children to learn this: to learn (1) that they cannot consistently accept and legitimize an authority, and then not obey it, and (2) that some people know more about certain things than they do, and that (given this) it is unreasonable not to accept what they say.

What is essential is to distinguish (1) and (2) from another thing which might perhaps be called 'authority' and is certainly in people's minds when they talk about 'authority':

3. The deployment of naked power, prestige, charisma, or 'moral pressure', when this is *not* legitimized as in (1) or (2) above. An 'authority' (better, someone who *pretends* to be an authority) in this sense attempts to gain obedience when there is no rationale for obedience. He says 'Do it because I say so' or 'because I'm your father' when these are not reasons for obeying. Similarly an elected team-captain has genuine authority, as in (1) above: the big bully in the team may influence others by his toughness and personality, but this is better termed 'influence' or 'power' or, at the most, '*de facto* authority' (if the team in fact obeys him rather than the elected captain).

If a child is to learn to accept (1) and (2), and to resist (3) wherever possible, he has somehow to learn the *conceptual* distinctions between them: to learn to *identify* particular cases of (1), (2) or (3). We have to educate him out of thinking solely in terms of 'obeying' or 'not obeying', 'conforming' or 'rebelling', and get him to distinguish between different *types* of obedience backed by different *reasons*. It is not, of course, likely that we can do this in as brief and direct a way as I have tried to do it above: that is, simply by pointing them out to him orally or on paper. We have therefore to instantiate these distinctions in different games, different social contexts, in order that he may see them for himself in action.

We need therefore not only (a) contexts or games which show only *one* of (1), (2) or (3) in operation, but also (b) contexts or games which show how one of them may get confused with another, with regrettable consequences. For example: suppose we play a game in which the group are given a certain task – say, to decorate and furnish their class-room. Assume that this task is voluntarily accepted by all the group, and that they are given some money to help carry it out. Now the group will need (1) certain of its members in positions of authority: if they think the context warrants it, they may choose a plenipotentiary leader, or they may form a committee, or they may discuss everything as equals and operate by common consent, merely appointing people to be in charge of specific tasks like accounting for the money they have been given. But to a greater or lesser extent, there will be contracted and legitimized authorities in sense (1). Secondly, one person will have had more experience of furniture-buying, or painting, or how to hang pictures. They will discover this and accept his authority in these areas (2). But also, unless the group is too strictly controlled, there will be certain members of the group who exercise a strong influence (3). This influence may work with the 'authorities' of (1) and (2), if for instance a member uses his strong personality and enthusiasm to further the task of the group: or it may work against them, if he 'sets a bad example', as in the case of the big bully in the team working against the captain.

All this is in essence very simple, and (in a sense) common knowledge to every teacher and indeed every pupil. What is important is that all of it should be made *explicit*. The importance of this game is not that the class-room gets decorated: it is that members of the group, the players, are enabled to become aware of what is happening in respect of (1), (2) and (3) – of how the concept of 'authority' is being attended to or disregarded during the task. To make it explicit, we can think of various methods – stopping the group directly after something has happened relevant to (1), (2) or (3) and commenting on it, discussing what has happened after the whole task is completed, advising at particular points before trouble arises, taking a tape-recording or a video-tape of the group during its performance and playing it back with discussion afterwards, appointing an 'outside' member of the group to write its 'history' in relation to authority, and so forth. I shall not comment on the merits or demerits of these and other techniques here; the purpose of the exercise should be plain enough.

C. PRACTICAL METHODS

If the points and logic that lie behind this kind of teaching are sufficiently clear, I shall not need to spend very much time on detailed descriptions of methods. In what follows I aim to do not much more than remind the teacher of certain practical moves that will necessarily follow from what we have noticed above.

I. RULES AND CONTRACTS WITHIN THE INSTITUTION

The authorities responsible for the rules of the institution will first of all ensure that these rules have a rational basis. This means, as we have seen, that they must not be first-order 'moralistic' rules, but must be justified by the function of the institution. In the case of each rule, the head teacher (or local education authority, or vice-chancellor, or principal, or whoever) must ask himself 'Is this rule required for the efficient functioning of this institution?'

The answer to this will not be directly given by reference to the will or the likes and dislikes of the head teacher himself, or the pupils' parents, or the pupils themselves, or the staff, or the governors, or the local authorities, or anything of that kind. It will be given by consideration of two classes of factors:

(i) What is required by (so to speak) 'pure reason', if there were no outside interference: what rules are in fact necessary for staff and pupils, if they are to teach and learn as effectively as possible.
(ii) What is required by public relations or (in a wide sense of the term) 'politics': that is, what is forced on the institution by the views of others and their power, however irrational.

An absolutely clear-cut distinction must be made, both in theory and practice, between these two. For instance, one might believe that certain rules about dress and manners were not required by (i): that learning would go on in the institution as efficiently, perhaps more efficiently, if the pupils were allowed to do what they liked in this area. But one might, under certain circumstances, also believe that these rules *were* required by (ii): that parents, or the town council, or some other body, insisted on certain standards of dress and manners, and would do the institution severe damage if these standards were not met.

Of course the person in authority has to weigh up such cases, balancing factors in (i) against factors in (ii). There is no determinate solution to all problems. What is important is that these quite different types of reason should be distinguished in the person's mind, *and presented to the pupils for what they are*. Thus if the only reason for having a particular rule is that the parents insist on it, and that this insistence must be met (otherwise perhaps they will withdraw their children, or not contribute to a new swimming-pool), then the authority must *say just this* to the pupils. Without this kind of honesty it will be very hard for the pupils to grasp the rationality of rules at all (and hard also for them to resist the impression that many adults are hypocritical).

How far the person in authority can or should resist irrational outside pressures is, again, a problem with no single solution. It is important that he should be neither over-awed by them, nor over-anxious to strike a blow for freedom which, however flamboyant, results in damage to his institution. He will find, however, that he can get away with a good deal provided his general public relations are good, and provided that he presents any changes that he wants to make in a manner which, while honest, is nevertheless most likely to gain acceptance. For instance, if he asks the parents of schoolchildren 'Is it all right if I tell the girls all about contraception, abortion clinics, sexual intercourse, etc. ?' they may well forbid this. Some will forbid it outright: others will, perhaps, cover their dislike by saying something like 'Only under approved conditions', 'Only if the school doctor does it', or whatever. (A high degree of rationality is not to be expected in this area.) On the other hand, if he says 'Educational experts seem to agree that we are failing our teenagers if we do not teach them about life: we are very shocked by their ignorance, permissiveness, immorality, etc.: so we hope to relieve you of some of this burden by 'learning to live' or 'moral education' courses – in which, of course, we shall try to banish their ignorance by teaching them the necessary facts about health, biology, personal hygiene, citizenship . . . etc.', then he may get nothing more than a few complaints as the course proceeds. (And if his teenagers are both loyal and discreet he may not even get that.)[1] In the same way, he may be unwise in actually handing out leaflets about contraception or V.D., but he may be able to have the relevant information in the school library – or at least information about where to get the information.

----

[1] This may seem ridiculously naïve. But I myself sent out two questionnaires to different 'generations' of parents, one cast in the first form, one in the second: both were honest representations of what I was going to tell the pupils, but the language used was different. The first produced about 80% of hostile replies: the second only about 5%. This was not a serious piece of research, so further details are not necessary.

But it is far from enough to make sure that the rules are rational, and present them to the pupils as such. The authorities must also:

(i) make sure that they carry specified sanctions with them, so that everybody can know exactly what the penalty is for breaking this or that rule:
(ii) make sure that the sanctions are actually enforced (preferably with a minimum of argument):
(iii) make sure that these rules and sanctions are, both individually and collectively, absolutely clearly specified, and understood by every pupil.

If this is done, it will save endless time and trouble: and above all, it will give practical shape to the crucial distinction between (1) having an established contract and set of rules which everybody agrees (however unwillingly) to keep, so that law and order is maintained and the institution can get on with the job, and (2) contexts in which argument about the rules is allowed and encouraged, pupils are taught to criticize rules, make up their own rules, and so forth. It is the blurring of this distinction which leads to the time-wasting, and sometimes the near-chaos, which is a feature of many contemporary institutions.

A vital point here, which we noticed in section B above, is the inclusion of second-order rules: that is, rules-about-changing-rules. These, like the first-order rules, must meet the criteria we have listed – they must be rationally based, rationally presented, and include specified and enforced sanctions. Thus the scope granted to different bodies (the school council, the student union, etc.) or to different methods (protests, demonstrations, strikes) in changing the rules must be clearly defined, and specific instances marked as legitimate or illegitimate. Whilst it is not possible here, any more than with the first-order rules, to specify *every* case in advance, it is both possible and desirable to specify as many as possible. Thus we may not want to say in advance whether a 'protest march' is acceptable or not: but we can at least specify anything which involves violence, disruption of traffic or normal work, or interference with other citizens, as illegitimate: as against (say) peaceful meetings in a park, against which we need make no special rules.

Provided all these distinctions are clearly observed, I do not think the authorities should have very much difficulty in determining the actual content of their rules. Thus we may feel reasonably certain that some things are absolutely necessary for almost any educational institution: there must be regular attendance, punctuality, absence of violence or other forms of disruption, and pupils must be in a fit state to do the work. This cuts out truancy, strikes, drunkenness, certain kinds of drug addiction, certain types of demonstration and disobedience, and so forth. Equally it would be hard to show that behaviour in the areas of sex, dress, hair-style, cosmetics, etc. were relevant to the institution. Of course it is always possible to dispute particular cases: some might say that school uniforms make the institution's work easier (keep the pupils' minds off the current fashions, avoid competition and jealousy between the rich and well-dressed girl and the poor Cinderella), whilst others might maintain the opposite (putting teenagers into uniform is repressive, makes them resent school, etc.). In such cases we may have to guess, or find out more facts. But provided the criteria are clear – provided we do not operate with some vague prejudicial notion of 'what is respectable' or 'what is permitted nowadays' – I do not think that reasonable people would disagree over many important cases.

The set of rules, or contract, which these criteria will generate apply, of course, only *for* the institution and only *within* the institution. The institution is part of a wider society, which has its own rules and sanctions. These will probably be hopelessly muddled, partly because our law-makers are not very bright: but the institution cannot help that; it can only try to educate the pupils in respect of the wider society, whilst clarifying and enforcing its own rules in a more coherent manner. It is the pupil's behaviour as a member of the institution, not as a citizen, with which we are here concerned. As with other institutions (clubs, societies), the pupils thus have (at least) two sets of rules to obey: the general rules of citizenship, and the specific contract which he enters into as a member of the particular institution. All this has to be made plain to the pupils.

Not all institutions, of course, set out to *educate*. Those that set out only to train for a particular purpose (e.g. a secretarial college) may, like other non-educational institutions, have no particular interest in framing those rules and contracts which are necessary for education in general, or for moral education in particular. But for educational institutions which are concerned (as I think most should be) with moral education, the kind of rules and contracts is likely to be significantly different. Thus we may well think it important[1] that pupils should be initiated into certain kinds of *tradition*,

[1] See R. S. Peters' essay in *Let's Teach Them Right* (ed. C. Macy: Pemberton Books).

involving behaviour not strictly required by the necessities of academic work. Here again, the elements of such traditions should not be a matter of our own likes and dislikes, but be judged by whether they contribute to the ends of moral education. Compulsory chapel services, or residence in a hall, or organized games, or morning assembly, *may* contribute to those ends, or they may not. We have to decide for ourselves: but we must decide on this criterion.

2. ACCEPTANCE OF THE CONTRACT

If the authorities of the institution have succeeded in carrying out the above simple suggestions, they will be able to present the pupils with a clear and detailed contract or set of contractual rules, each backed by a solid argument of the appropriate type. This in itself would be a big step forward. But it is not enough. The authorities must secure *acceptance* of the contract.

'Acceptance' here – and this must be made plain to the pupils – does *not* mean absolute agreement: that is, the pupil does not have to think that all the rules are right, or even that many of them are. To accept the contract means to have, and declare, the sincere intention of keeping the rules – whatever one's opinion may be about their merits. This in turn involves agreement that sanctions should be applied if one does break a rule, and the intention of making restitution so far as possible. If these were not involved, we should not say that a person had sincerely accepted the contract.

What the authorities should say to the pupils, then, is something like this: 'You are going to be a member of this institution. Here are the rules, about which we've thought a great deal, and which we think we can justify to the satisfaction of most reasonable people' (and at some point the rules and justifications would be gone through in detail): 'now, you may still think that some of them are silly: we shall give you plenty of opportunity to say so, and say why you think so: and there are various mechanisms for changing the rules, in which you can take part' (these also gone through in detail). 'Of course we don't anticipate that you'll keep all the rules all the time: we are all of us swayed by emotion, selfish, forgetful, etc.: but granted all this, do you accept the rules and contract? Do you promise to abide by them? Will you consider yourself bound by them? Or is your attitude rather that you feel justified in breaking some of them if you can get away with it?'

Of course this sounds naïve; but it will, I hope, at least give some impression of what the authorities have to get across. Some general

methods of getting the concept of rules across are considered later
on: here I would simply advise that the authorities should (1)
present this contract *before* the pupils become members of the
institution, (2) continue to present it at regular intervals, (3) have
some kind of formal ceremony at which the pupils indicate their
acceptance, and actually inscribe their signature on the contract,
(4) use the signed contracts when any rule is subsequently broken
by the pupil, to remind him in concrete form of what his agreement
was. No doubt other methods will suggest themselves to the teacher.

There is naturally a difference, in degree if not in kind, between
those institutions at which attendance is compulsory (schools) and
at which it is not (universities). In the latter case, we can say to the
students words to the effect of 'Look, you don't *have* to come here,
so if you want to come we must be quite sure that you agree to our
rules', etc. In the former we cannot say this. If a schoolboy below
the school-leaving age says to us 'This is very unfair: I'm compelled
to agree, because I'm compelled to be a member of this institution',
what can we reply? We should say something like 'Yes, you are
compelled: but this is inevitable. In this society, where you happen
to have had the good or bad luck to be born, you cannot survive
below a certain age, unless you are at school. Whether this is the
right way to run a society may be disputed; but we think it is right,
and if you think it is wrong you must persuade enough people to
change it in due course. Meanwhile, we are not just compelling you
for our own amusement: we teach you, feed you, look after your
health, and so on. Given all this, and things as they actually are, do
you not think it reasonable to agree to the contract?'

He may still say – or think – that he is not going to agree. We then
have to say 'Very well, I see that you still think it unfair. But now
you have a choice. You have got to keep the rules to some extent
anyway, because you are outnumbered, and force is on our side. Do
you want to keep them voluntarily – even if you think it in principle
unfair: or would you rather be in a permanent state of war with us?
We do not ask you to agree with all the rules, or even any of them:
nor do we ask you to think that you are getting a fair deal. All we ask
is that you form the intention of keeping the rules. If you don't
form this intention, then we on our side are entitled to regard you as
an enemy: and we should be entitled also – though we may not
actually do this – to withdraw the benefits which make up our side
of the bargain. If you are not willing even to try to keep the rules,
why should we be willing to feed you, house you, look after you

when you are ill, and so forth? Perhaps on reflection, or after some experience in which society did not support you in this way, you will change your mind'.

This is a last-ditch defence. If after this we still have people who are not going to agree, we should have to decide what to do. Arguably we might in fact withdraw from our side of the bargain, and cut off supplies until they come to their senses: at the least we should mark them down, in some formal way, as actual or potential enemies of the system – in effect, as outlaws. For that is what they are: that is how they have positioned themselves, and the only educational move left to us is to show them the natural consequences of so positioning themselves. To try to cover this up, to pretend to ourselves and to them that they are still good contractual members of the institution, is merely to deceive everybody. They are parasitical, and must be shown to be such. Only a vague fear of being labelled 'authoritarian' or 'tough-minded' could prevent us from taking such measures.

As I have written it here, all these moves are bound to seem oversimplified: and it must be understood that almost everything depends on the way in which they are made – on the teacher-pupil relationships in general, the home background, and so forth. All this we know already. But it is no excuse for shirking the task of trying to bring out, in some clearly formalized way, the logical points that underlie such moves.

3. SANCTIONS AND PUNISHMENT

In the last two sections (1 and 2), I have tried to say something about (1) the necessity for framing, communicating and enforcing a clearly-defined contract, and (2) the arguments which might be used to persuade pupils to adopt it. But to some people in some institutions, our discussion of rules and contracts may seem somewhat academic: the educators may have difficulty in maintaining even a minimum of law and order. So it is worth taking a close look at the notions of sanctions and punishment.

(a) First, it is important that the teacher has the right view of punishment to begin with. Specific punishments, sanctions or penalties are unpleasant things which are meted out by the authorities to people living in a rule-governed system, for specific breaches of the rules: it is part of the concept of a rule, in such a system, that a penalty normally follows the breaking of it – if it did not, there would be no rule but just a pious hope. So we must not look on punishment as something which a 'progressive' or 'liberal' teacher would avoid because it is unpleasant or nasty – it is *meant to be* nasty. That is what punishment is: and that is what you have to have if there are to be rules at all. Equally, punishment must not stem from the vindictive or angry feelings of the teacher or other authority. It is nothing to do with his (or the pupils') feelings at all: it is simply a logical consequence of rule-breaking.

(b) This essential *impersonality* of punishment must be communicated to the pupils, so that they do not have the excuse of pretending that punishment is just 'them', the authorities, taking it out of 'us', the pupils. Obviously the more the authorities can cooperate with the pupils in framing the contract and the sanctions, the better. They can say in effect 'Look, let's see what rules we need: O.K., we need rules X, Y and Z: now, we all know that we are often impulsive, angry, selfish, lazy and so on: so what punishments do we need to attach to these rules to make sure they *are* rules, to make sure they are kept?' (Often the pupils will make better suggestions than the teachers.) Then when rules are broken, the teacher will not have to pose as a flouted authority, a person or pseudo-god whose will has been challenged: that is to play into the hands of the pupils' own immaturity. We have somehow to get them past the stage of conducting mimic battles, of rebelling against 'authority' in the shape of father-figures who have to be challenged. We have to avoid taking the role which the pupils' immaturity wants us to take, the role of the irate parent. We have rather to say something like 'Oh, gosh, you've broken such-and-such a rule, what a pity you couldn't keep it: well, now, that means you have to do or suffer so-and-so, as we agreed in the contract, doesn't it?' Of course it is equally important that at *other* times, i.e. when not simply enforcing the contract, the teacher should appear (so to speak) more as a human being – as someone who *is* sometimes angry, gets bored or resentful, though for most of the time (I hope) is quite fond of his pupils and will relate to them, be trusted by them and so on. The important thing is to *dissociate* the contract-system from these personal considerations: our pupils have to learn that rules and punishments are necessary, *not* because adults want them, but because any form of human life logically requires them. Just as we distinguish between the judge as a person and the judge as a law-enforcer, so they must learn to distinguish between the teacher as a person and the teacher in his role as rule-keeper or umpire.

(c) The specific forms of punishment that we choose must, of course, be effective in ensuring that the rules are kept; and it is for this reason that they must be unpleasant. (If they were pleasant, breaking the rules would be rewarded, and they would no longer be rules forbidding so-and-so, but rules encouraging people to do so-and-so.) What precise forms of punishment are effective in this way, for what types of people, is of course an empirical question on which I cannot pronounce. All that is important here is to keep *this* mode of dealing with pupils – the mode of *deterring* – clearly distinct from other modes. For instance, as well as deterring a person we should also want him to make restitution, since as we saw earlier the sincere acceptance of a contract involves a person's being willing to make up for the damage or trouble he has caused by breaking it. But what we should say is not 'You have deliberately broken Johnny's watch, which cost him a lot of money and trouble to get: I'll punish you by making you buy a new one'. For here we have muddled up two modes. Making him buy a new one may be no good as a deterrent: maybe the pupil is rich enough not to care, or if he is really sorry, he may genuinely want to make up for it by buying a new one. What we should say is 'You've deliberately broken his watch: now, by the rules, you must be deterred in some way to stop you doing that sort of thing again' (and here perhaps we beat him or do something else which he doesn't like): 'and, which is quite different, since it's your fault Johnny's not got a watch any more, the least you can do is to buy him a new one'. Both these can be enforced, but they are different. Again, if a pupil is grossly lazy and consequently gets behind in his work, we want him (i) to stop being lazy, and (ii) to catch up with his work. It *may* be that keeping him in detention does both of these: but not necessarily. We have to be clear what we are doing.

Armed with this clarity, by which he can translate his practical knowledge and experience into effectiveness, the teacher should find it easier both to maintain discipline and to communicate the rules-and-contract system to his pupils. Nevertheless, much of what I have said may still seem very impractical. A teacher, particularly if he is teaching in a 'tough' or badly-disciplined school, may be disposed to say 'It's all very well telling us to enforce this contract, but *how*? We're often not allowed to apply certain sanctions (for instance corporal punishment): indeed sometimes we can't defend ourselves against some young thugs. Again, you tell us to persuade them to accept the contract: but some of them just *won't*, and what are we to do then? If we make all these rules and contracts very clear, as you suggest, and then can't enforce them, won't we just look sillier than ever?'

These are very fair points. I do indeed believe that the clarity, and the moves I have been recommending, would reduce the brute problem of maintaining law and order: particularly if this approach were adopted towards children from their earliest years. But I am not starry-eyed enough to believe that there will not be resisting cases. About these I can only add the following:

(d) We are talking here (as at the end of section 2) about pupils who are, quite overtly and deliberately, opposed to the institution and its teachers: who have not made the move of accepting any sort of contract: who are predisposed not to agree, or to obey, at all. It is important that the teacher should identify these cases clearly, and not confuse them with the quite different cases of pupils who do, basically, accept the contract, but (for various psychological reasons) find it difficult to keep. But it is equally important for the teacher, once having identified them, to be clear that this is, in effect, war: and a war which the teachers cannot afford to lose. They cannot afford to lose, not only (i) because there is chaos in the school and teaching suffers, or (ii) because the particular contract that defines the school as an institution is being flouted, but (iii) because this is, for the pupil, a model or archetypal case; and his attitude to and understanding of other future contracts will be determined by what happens to him here. Thus it is strictly for educational reasons, not just considerations of convenience, that the pupils must not be allowed to get away with it. Hence there is one move the teacher must not make: he must not back down, accept defeat, make some sort of compromise for the sake of a quiet life, or pretend the problem does not exist.

(e) If it is war, what weapons does the teacher have? I omit here the various common sanctions that are used: detention, reporting to the headmaster and so forth. We are to assume that other sanctions or pseudo-sanctions which the teacher may summon up, such as the pressure of the peer group or the backing of the pupils' parents, do not work either: nor anything the teacher can do by way of informal relations with the pupil, in or out of school: nor anything the official experts (the educational psychologist, the probation officer, etc.) can do. Next we assume that certain types of sanctions, which the teacher thinks might work (e.g. corporal punishment), are forbidden by the (possibly misguided) higher authorities. Finally we assume that the teacher cannot ensure that the recalcitrant pupils are removed from the school, and sent to some other institution. There remain two general lines of action:

(i) The teacher, with the cooperation of the other teachers, can invent new sanctions of a different type. He can say 'Look, I just cannot do my job, because I am not allowed to enforce certain rules, rules which I consider to be absolutely essential for any effective teaching, on certain pupils. Very well: I regard these pupils as wholly at war with us. If I can, I shall make sure that they pass no examinations: and also that they are regarded as unemployable – we are preparing a 'black list' of such pupils, which we shall circulate to employers and others. If the state or other authorities force me to make certain moves, such as standing in front of a class and teaching them, allowing them to sit for examinations, etc., then I shall make these moves: but I will do it in the most inefficient and incompetent manner possible. Anyway, I assure you that, if I am not given the necessary powers, parental backing, etc., these pupils will certainly suffer in their careers: very likely they may become real criminals, in which case they will be a burden on society in general and the police in particular'. I have no doubt that clear-headed and determined teachers, acting in cooperation, could make this work effectively.

(ii) The school can simply arrange that the pupils who are at war should spend the whole of the time under conditions different from the other pupils. This would, in effect, be to produce a 'detention wing', or a mini-Borstal, within the school: something which, if the higher authorities will not arrange outside the school, teachers can arrange for themselves.

All this would, of course, be highly regrettable: and naturally nobody wants it to come to that. We should hope that, by clarity in rule-making, by participation, by kindness, good staff-pupil relationships, parental support, etc, such cases would not arise. But – and it is a big 'but' – it is better that they should be seen to arise, and be dealt with along these lines, than that we should pretend that they do not exist. It is far from uncommon – even in the 'best' schools – for there to be a sort of muted war between staff (or one or two members of the staff) and pupils (or some pupils). This must, at all costs, be brought into the open rather than muffled.

We have to remember that we are talking only about *one* mode of dealing with our pupils. None of what I have suggested here should be taken as implying that we should not *also* adopt the methods of the friend, the elder brother, or even the psychotherapist as well as those of the judge and the policeman. Naturally, if the former methods are effectively deployed, the latter will be unnecessary. But both are valid. The important thing is to keep them distinct, and to use them both with a clear understanding. If this is clear, we may now turn our attention to the general educational methods which may help pupils to grasp these points – and which, we may hope, might obviate some of the more extreme difficulties we have been considering.

4. RULE–AND–CONTRACT TEACHING IN GENERAL

(a) *General methodology.* In Part II of this book we looked at what we called the 'discussion-form': and much of what was said there is relevant to the teaching of rules and contracts in general. It is helpful to regard rule-and-contract systems as being in certain important respects like games (though the analogy breaks down at some points): particularly perhaps for children, who are more familiar with the notion of a game than the wider notion of a contract. The game analogy is especially useful in helping the pupils to grasp some of the points made in earlier sections of this Part, e.g. (i) the *variety* of possible contracts (ii) the idea that contracts and rule-governed activities have a *purpose*, (iii) the rules can be changed to carry out the purpose more efficiently, (iv) various points about 'authority', and so forth. So I do not think the teacher should hesitate to use the analogy to the full.

There will be three basic types of context in which the teacher will try to get these points across:

(1) An '*academic*' context, in which the points are made in a general form – perhaps roughly in the way I have made them here, suitably altered for different kinds of pupils.
(2) The use of *examples*: either 'real-life' examples, or simulation situations, illustrations from the pupil's own experience (e.g. is there a 'contract' in his family life?) or a study of examples from history, legal cases, and actual contracts (e.g. between worker and employer).
(3) A context of *participation*. Here the pupils take part in framing and keeping contracts and sets of rules (e.g. as a school council, in arranging a dance or an outing, etc.).

I want to stress that all these are important, and none sufficient by itself. (3) is perhaps especially to be encouraged in schools and other institutions, because it is only in a participation-situation that pupils will clearly see the 'pay-off' – the actual results of making or breaking particular rules. It is essential to put responsibility firmly on the pupils themselves: otherwise it really *does* become no more than a game to them, in the sense that it is not taken seriously. (This is, of course, the merit especially claimed for such methods as those used by the Outward Bound authorities, the 'summer camps' in the U.S.A., and so on.) But equally, unless (1) and (2) are also used, the learning that is supposed to accrue from such situations will not be generalized, and hence not transferred to other rule-governed situations. (A boy may see the point of rules in mountain-climbing, but not necessarily be helped thereby to see the point of rules in school or factory.) The 'academic' or conceptual teaching, together with 'real-life' examples, literary illustrations, acted-out situations, etc., is essential if the pupils are to develop true under-standing.[1]

(b) *Contexts and examples.* The 'academic' points ((1) above) have been made in this book. I list here a random selection of contexts and examples for use in (2) and (3):

1. Non-directive out-of-school situations, not centred on a particular task, in which a great deal of responsibility is placed on pupils for building social rules virtually from scratch (e.g. summer camps, survival situations, 'desert island' situations – cf. William Golding's *Lord of the Flies* – and so on).

2. Specific out-of-school tasks which the pupils can be responsible for (school outings, arranging entertainments, organizing voluntary service, running a shop or a small-scale business enterprise).

3. In-school situations where pupils can be given practice in organizing and participating (the actual teaching/learning of a subject, school assembly, school councils, arrangements for catering, cleaning, decorating, repairing, building, etc.).

4. Simulated situations or games that can be played (a) with a particular task in mind for the group (e.g. a murder trial, con-ducting a political campaign), and (b) with no particular group-function, but concentrating rather on the political and social rules which the group may evolve (the 'desert island' case).

---

[1] See pp. 98–100.

5. Descriptions and discussion of (a) clear, and (b) problematic, cases of contract-keeping and contract-breaking, in history or literature or law.

6. Use of a wide variety of different contexts requiring different rules, particularly those varying on the dimension between 'instant obedience' and 'democratic discussion' (e.g. being in the army, serving as the crew of a sailing-ship, or as a nurse, on the one hand: being on a committee or deciding something with one's friends on the other). Role-playing in these different contexts is an obvious technique here.

7. Exchanging roles, particularly those which the pupil finds it difficult to grasp in the abstract, or about which he has prejudices (e.g. making the pupil act as the teacher, the foreman, the janitor, a policeman, etc.).

8. Accustoming the pupil to different social rituals or conventions (an old-fashioned dance, an unusual religious service, etc.).

9. Accustoming the pupil to different power-structures (dictatorship, oligarchy, etc.) in a context which is a microcosm of such regimes.

10. Accustoming the pupil to different decision-procedures (throwing dice, obeying a single person, voting, letting the most vocal or the strongest have their own way, etc.).

(c) *What the pupil must notice.* Here is a selection of questions which the pupil should be encouraged to raise and answer in all these contexts and in such others as the teacher may devise:

1. In this (rule-governed) situation, where does the authority lie? In the will of a person or group? In written rules? Unwritten expectations?

2. What, in detail, *are* the rules governing this situation?

3. What sanctions attach to them? Are these specified, or do they consist in the general disapproval of other people? Are the sanctions enforced?

4. Are any of the rules ambiguous or vague? Is it clear what is to count as (e.g.) 'obscene' or 'tending to corrupt'?

5. Do the rules fulfil their purpose? Are they reasonable and requisite?

6. What is the *point* of this 'game' or rule-governed system? Is it something we engage in for its own sake, like a real game, or is it supposed to result in some kind of product (as discussions are

supposed to result in truth, or social rules to result in social convenience)?

7. How would one make restitution for breaches of particular rules? What sort of damage is done by such breaches? What is the expenditure of time or trouble?

8. What temptation does one feel to break rule X or Y?

9. What temptation does one feel to dislike the rules in general, and rebel against them? Or to be over-anxious in conforming to them?

10. In rule-*making*, what temptation does one feel towards excessive strictness or excessive laxity?

I shall not repeat here all I have said, in describing the other methods in Parts I and II, about the importance of the teacher using his own imagination, monitoring and objectifying all these teaching-situations by video-tape, etc., making sure that the conceptual points are fully understood, and so forth. I shall confine myself to pleading with him to be imaginative and bold, indeed, but also at all costs to be *definite*. Here too we are up against a good deal of fashionable chit-chat about 'participation', 'pupil power', 'the democratic school', 'student protest' and so forth, which is as vague as it is boring. There is little point merely in encouraging the pupils to 'join in' or 'participate': if it is not clear to them what they are supposed to be learning, some of the more sensible ones will prefer to stick to their academic text-books. Boldness is required primarily in using new contexts of teaching (for instance, out-of-school non-directive situations, rather than academic discussion): but the teacher then needs to go back again and again over the particular context, discussing it, making the pupils 're-play' it, recording it, having outside observers comment on it, and so on. We must ensure that the pupils are not just having a good (or bad) time. We owe it to them that they should learn.

PART IV

The School Community

This Part is intended for teachers, educational administrators, parents and all those who are concerned with what the school, as a social organization, can do about moral education. It is intended to be 'practical' rather than 'academic'; and as it is not a serious essay in sociology or social psychology, I need make no apologies to professional social scientists. I have learned something from studying their researches (though not as much as I had hoped); but this whole area needs more study. Nevertheless, there is quite a lot of practical value that can be said.

A. EDUCATIONAL AND OTHER OBJECTIVES[1]

As it stands, the social organization of the school is not very much concerned with 'education' in a strict sense at all. The term can be loosely used to mean something like 'whatever goes on in schools, universities, etc.'. But this usage *is* loose; and it is not hard to think of things that go on in schools that we should not, on reflection, want to call 'education'. We make sure that the children's teeth are sound, that they eat a good lunch, that they are not run over in the street during school hours: all these are important, but they are not education. For in these cases the pupils' *knowledge* and *rationality* are not being developed. They are not *learning* or *being taught* anything.

Similarly much of what is said and written about 'education', including a great deal of so-called 'educational research', is not about education in our sense at all. It is about *other* things that have to do with educational institutions. If I talk about the cost of school buildings, or the country's need for more technologists, or the social injustice of segregation in secondary schools, I am not (at least, not directly) talking about any process of teaching and learning. Of

[1] On the concept of education see R. S. Peters, *Ethics and Education*, Part I.

D

course some of these (non-educational) matters may be very important. It does not follow that features of the school which have little or nothing to do with education must always take second place to the strictly educational features. All that follows is that the educational and non-educational aspects are importantly *different*.

But we should be bound to find it regrettable if educational institutions found little time for educating – or, to put it another way, if they ceased to be *educational* institutions. I say 'bound', because it is part of the concept of education that the educated person is in some way *improved* by being educated (we should not call it education if he were not). Education, then, is something which must (logically) receive the support and approval of all men, whatever their particular beliefs or values: something we wish to defend, and encourage so far as practical pressures allow.

It follows from this that we wish to defend and encourage education *not* for extrinsic or utilitarian reasons (e.g. to get more technologists, to keep our pupils off the streets or improve their social chances), but for its own sake. For if not, it would not be *education* that we were defending and encouraging. This is not to say that there are not good reasons why it is important to develop pupils' knowledge and rationality – of course there are. It is to say only that the kind of reasons is important. If our objectives are cast in such forms as 'to give everyone an equal chance to make money', or 'to fit children for their society', or 'to reduce juvenile delinquency', or 'to produce more technologists', we shall find ourselves defending not *education* as such, but certain social institutions, or certain skills and forms of training that may be useful, or other things that have no necessary connection with the development of reason and awareness.

In the case of 'moral education', I have already given a definition and a break-down of aims earlier, and need not repeat it at this point. But, to use this example, it is clear that anyone who thought that the aims of moral education were primarily to prevent certain forms of behaviour, to give the police less work, to indoctrinate citizens in obeying the state, etc. would not be talking about aims of moral *education* at all. Of course it is to be hoped (and predicted) that effective moral education will – incidentally – achieve such aims. But that is not what 'moral education' *means*. The morally educated person is one who has developed certain forms of rationality – knowledge, skills, attitudes and principles – which are required for good performance in the area we call 'moral'.

I want now to look briefly at some of these other, non-educational things which schools and colleges may be doing: chiefly in order that the reader may be aware of them and be able to lay them on one side.

1. First, they may simply be keeping their pupils 'in play': that is, under supervision, off the streets and the labour market, out of the way of the adult world and in comparative safety.

2. They may be used to inculcate the pupils with the particular behaviour-patterns required by their society: for instance, to give children the kind of 'responsibility' which their parents want them to have.

3. They may be used to enable their pupils to survive economically (or to do well economically) in society: or to give them a chance of raising their social class.

4. They may be used to train pupils for tasks which society requires (war, technology, etc.).

5. They may be used to select pupils for entry into other educational establishments (e.g. the university).

These and other functions have been discussed at length by professional sociologists. Our interest in them as educators is only partial. We have to appreciate their importance, and bear it in mind when planning our schools and colleges: for otherwise our planning may be impractical. But above all, we need to be clear when researchers or administrators ask us to do this or that under the title of 'education': for usually what they are asking for is one or the other of 1–5 above, and not anything to do with education in our sense at all. They are entitled to ask for it, and we have to see the force of the requests. But we must not muddle them up with education.

It is a fairly safe bet that statesmen (politicians) and other administrators will not have much time to spare for education in our sense. The present title of the relevant ministry in the U.K. – the 'Department of Education *and Science*' – makes the point by itself. Rightly or wrongly (and this depends on the circumstances), they will concern themselves with pressing national issues. Are we getting enough scientists? Will the supply of teachers be sufficient? Are the working classes getting a fair chance of social success? How about the public (elsewhere, private) schools in the light of social justice? These will be the sort of questions that they will be concerned with. If a decision has to be made about (say) religious education, it is likely to be made not upon the proper philosophical and educational grounds, but (at least partly) upon the desires and fears of various pressure groups and churches: that is, it will be a political rather than (if I may so put it) a rational decision.

I do not, of course, want to deny that there is some (small) scope in politics for serious educational thought. But one must not expect it; and this places a great burden upon the educators themselves – on the philosophers, psychologists and others who conduct research into education, and above all on the *teachers*. Some countries, like the U.K., are on the whole fairly fortunate in not being over-controlled by state or local authorities: and there is a good deal that teachers can do. It is important that they realize that the *educational* side of their work is chiefly their responsibility. To look to governmental authorities for any serious lead in this direction is an error. (By a 'serious' lead, I of course exclude the vague generalities and admonishments made in state-sponsored reports by various committees and commissions, whose task is usually more political than rational.)

Every now and then a voice will be heard in the educational world which actually talks about *education*. Such voices will be frequent in training colleges and university departments, and some of them will be ancient – Plato, Aristotle, Locke, Rousseau, Dewey, and so on. Less frequently they are heard in everyday life, sometimes coming from people who have actually managed to influence the course of events to a greater or lesser extent – Froebel, Steiner, Montessori, Isaacs, Neill. In the case of moral education, there is a (somewhat dubious) tradition, one strand of which runs from Plato to Sir Richard Livingstone.

These people are usually found to protest – rightly – against the excessive attention paid to the other, non-educational functions of schools and colleges. But the writers on moral education, at least, have usually suffered from disadvantages which have rendered their work inoperative. First, they have been vague. It is not much use talking generally about 'the importance of excellence', 'the all-round man', 'the best of human thought and art': or, to be more contemporary, 'concern', 'awareness', 'sensitivity', 'spiritual values' and so on. Secondly, they have been partisan: they have based their morality on the ideals of a particular class, creed or culture. And thirdly, they have not made many practical suggestions about how teachers should actually set about this task in schools.

Nevertheless, they are right to protest; and they are at least talking about education. What I want to stress here is not just that the responsibility for turning their protests into action rests with the practical educators and teachers: but that the educators and teachers should consider that responsibility as something that they are bound to do something about, if they have any interest in education. If they consider themselves as paid civil servants, trades unionists, ushers, hired tutors, pipe-lines for 'social values' or 'social mobility', or anything of the kind, then the future of education is grim indeed. Of course it is understandable that teachers should feel themselves in this (degraded) position. They are not paid overmuch: they are pestered and dictated to by bureaucrats: they are overworked: their professional status is inadequate. It may be as much as most teachers can do to survive and earn a reasonable living. But one hopes for more.

I personally hope for so much more that I should like to see teachers and educators in control of administrators, rather than vice versa. This also seems to follow from the notion of education. We may readily grant that there are certain (non-educational) objectives that the state may thrust upon us: if the country needs technologists or soldiers in order to survive, we have to satisfy that need. But there will be *some* area – one would hope, a fairly large one – where the aims and objectives are strictly educational. And here the 'experts', in so far as there are any experts, will be found amongst researchers, the teachers, and practical educators; certainly not among the administration.

It is an old point, but of crucial importance, that 'administration' tends to take over (even to multiply itself) unless power is in the hands of the relevant people. In the case of a business firm, this is easier to arrange: for if the business does not (say) actually sell enough oil, it goes broke – and the administration of the business will be geared to selling sufficient. In the case of educational institutions, the aim (some of the time) is to educate. Those who know best how to do this must be able to control whatever para-phernalia is necessary to make their jobs easier – administration, architecture, money, equipment and so forth. More important for our own purposes in this book, they must be able to control the *social arrangements* of the school.

For various reasons – partly the (apparent) stranglehold of the system, but partly also through inertia – teachers tend to accept the social forms of the school as 'given'. Those who feel strongly, for instance, about the importance of a 'house system', or 'progressive' schooling, or 'tradition', will naturally gravitate to schools of a suitable type. The implication is that those that remain are satisfied with things as they are. But this is not so. Many teachers are no doubt uncertain about *what* social changes are required in schools where they teach; but I have met few who are uncertain that *some* such changes are badly needed. Their complaints are not always about shorter hours and better pay. They are aware that moral education depends very much on the social context, and they are aware that moral education is of central importance to their pupils. Where there appears to be apathy, it is the apathy produced by being forced – as it seems to them – to accept the system: not the apathy of those whose concern for education is minimal.

For there can be few teachers who have not experienced the reward, not only of sparking off interest or clarity concerning a school subject, but also of making some impression on their pupils as *people*: on their moral development, their emotions, their inner judgements and outward behaviour. And there will be even fewer who have not felt the frustration of *not* being able to do this more often: due sometimes, perhaps, to their own deficiencies, but at least as often to shortage of time, pressure of work, or the sheer inefficiency of the social arrangements of the school.

Most teachers are probably aware that the aims of moral education cannot be adequately met by curricular methods alone. Of our 'moral components', which are a convenient way of representing those aims, it seems that only GIG, perhaps EMP, and the more cognitive or 'intellectual' aspects of PHIL lend themselves to teaching over the desk-tops. And though, as I have said elsewhere,[1] much may be gained by the use of such methods as role-play, drama, music, simulation situations and so forth, I do not need to stress the general importance of the social context in which these occur, and of the school as a whole. The greater part of PHIL, and the crucially important components KRAT(1) and (2), are unlikely to be developed except in a suitable social context.

What we shall be doing in this Part is to develop, in a more practical and detailed form, some suggestions which seem likely (partly on *a priori* grounds, partly as a result of teachers' own experience, and partly from research findings) to be valid in this area. Some of these were made in a very brief form elsewhere:[2] here we shall add to and expand them. I ask two things of the reader. First, to bear constantly in mind the fact that we are dealing with *education*,

---

[1] *I.M.E.*, pp. 411-12.
[2] *I.M.E.*, pp. 409-11.

not with other requirements: we shall see later how our suggestions can be made to fit in with the latter, but we badly need, to begin with, a clear picture of what we want *as educators*. Second, to clear the decks of his mind for a general approach to the problem. Some readers will be very familiar with the sort of suggestions made, though perhaps as part of a different tradition: others will regard them as surprising or unusual. Both need to step back from their own experience, and look at the matter as a whole.

B. MORAL EDUCATION – 'ACADEMIC' OR 'SOCIAL'?

The intelligent reader, if asked whether moral education should be done by 'academic' methods (classroom periods) or 'social' arrangements (creating a good 'atmosphere' in the school), would dismiss the question as silly. He would say, rightly, that we need both. But before we dismiss it, we need to understand fully why it is silly. For on this understanding depends our grasp of what *kind* of benefits we can expect from new social arrangements in schools, and how these benefits connect with more 'academic' learning.

First, it is worth remembering that there are many not-so-intelligent readers or non-readers who would *not* dismiss the question as silly, but would answer it along various doctrinaire lines. Some, apparently regarding the word 'education' as virtually synonymous with 'what goes on in the classroom', will be inclined to suppose that 'moral education' must, somehow, be some form of classroom instruction: rather like 'R.E.' or 'R.I.' periods, but (we hope) better. They think, perhaps, in terms of discussions about controversial moral issues: teaching important facts about the law, or old people, or war, or sex, or air pollution: or 'bringing morals into' other already-established classroom subjects, such as history or literature. Others, who seem to think that morality is something that (in some mysterious way) *rubs off* on children, will tend to assume that nothing important can be done by direct teaching. It is all a matter of 'setting a good example', 'having the right sort of tradition', 'a good school atmosphere', etc.

The positive suggestions of both these groups may be very sensible; but it is fatally easy to be wedded to *one* particular approach – and to remain wedded, even though one may be forced to admit in argument that both are necessary. Often what lies behind such doctrinaire thinking is some (perhaps unconscious) *model* of 'how children learn to be moral': a model which would not survive a firm grasp of our very various 'moral components'. For instance, there are those who suppose that children learn primarily by *example* : if they have 'good men' (teachers) to imitate, all will be well. Others suppose that morality is essentially like factual knowledge, and can be taught like it: there are certain 'moral laws', which perhaps we can elucidate by dressing them up in fables or stories (' . . . and the moral of *that* is, "Do as you would be done by" '). Others again seem to believe that particular experiences or locales exert a strong influence in themselves: put your pupils on board a sailing ship, or on a mountaineering expedition, or amid the flowers and fields of nature, and moral virtue will somehow flow into him ('If a man can tackle a mountain he can tackle Life').

Some of these pictures may seem obviously old-fashioned or naïve; but the doctrinaire tendency persists just as strongly in contemporary educational fashion. I will give three examples of this:

1. Many writers identify the *'authoritarian role'* of the teacher as the chief obstacle to moral learning and development. The claim is that teachers are perceived by pupils as 'authorities' who dictate beliefs and values to them *ex cathedra*: whereas what the teachers ought to be doing is to act in a more 'permissive', 'democratic', 'liberal' or 'egalitarian' way, not in an 'authoritarian role'. Some seem even to maintain that, in the course of discussion on moral problems, the teacher should not express his own views at all, but act as a 'neutral chairman'. The pupils should not be given 'right answers', but encouraged to adopt their own moral values by their own thought-processes and exchange of argument.

Of course, in morality as in any other field of rational thought and action, our objective is to develop the pupils' autonomy.[1] Simply giving the 'right answers' is as educationally inadequate here as it is in the field of mathematics (where the pupil could look them up for himself at the back of the textbook). But it does not follow from this that the teacher has no 'rational authority', or that he should never adopt an 'authoritarian role'. Indeed, if we are to talk seriously of moral *education*, then our objective will partly be to teach the pupils to think in certain (reasonable) ways, and not in certain other (unreasonable) ways. If we do not at least have a clear idea of an appropriate *methodology* – roughly, a right way of 'doing morals' – and a clear idea of success and failure in morality, then we have no business to attempt moral education at all. Our discussions will be

[1] *I.M.E.*, Chapters 1 and 2.

mere free-for-alls, with no question of *truth* or *correctness* or *rationality* at stake. As with other forms of thought, the teacher has of course to get the pupils to think, rather than merely obey: but he has to get them to think in a certain style, and in accordance with certain rules and criteria.

In terms of our moral components: the pupil must naturally make up his own mind about what is right and wrong – if he does not, words like 'right', 'wrong', 'ought', etc. will lack prescriptive force, and simply mean for him 'what teacher expects' or 'what society wants': and this will not develop his KRAT(1) – his judgements will not translate themselves into effective decision and action. Equally the pupil must see for himself the reasons which make concern for others (PHIL) a justifiable moral principle. But on the other hand, these reasons have to be *taught*: and there must be some 'authority' to teach them – that is, somebody who is clear about what they are and good at passing them on to pupils. More obviously, relevant facts about moral situations (GIG) or about the feelings of others (EMP) may be more clearly understood by 'authorities' than by laymen.[1]

Hence both in morality and other areas of education it is silly to ask such questions as 'Should the teacher play an "authoritarian" or a "democratic" role?' For the obvious answer is that he should play *many different* roles. Everything depends on what is being taught, on what sort of context the teaching and learning demands. It is equally ridiculous to suggest that I can lecture on the facts about air pollution or the psychology of race prejudice without being in some sense 'authoritarian', as to suggest that I can join in a seminar-discussion among equals without being in some sense 'egalitarian' or 'democratic'. A glance at the list of moral components is enough to show that these and many other contexts are required, so that many roles are required to fit them.

2. Some claim that only *'real life' experiences* are effective in moral learning: that anything 'artificial', or which does not 'stem from the child's immediate concern' or 'arise from the child's life-situation' will never work. The pupil 'learns by living': 'life and experience are the true teachers'. This is an understandable reaction against certain highly artificial or old-fashioned types of education, but it will not do as a general theory.

If we took it seriously, we should not set out to *educate* the child at all. We should simply let him live and have experiences. In fact, of

[1] *I.M.E.*, pp. 100–1.

course, we *control* his experiences in such a way that the child learns to reflect on them, understand them, and adopt certain rules and principles in relation to them. All this we know perfectly well already; and we can only understand the theory under discussion if we take it to be emphasising the importance of certain criteria in relation to our control of the child's experiences – briefly, that the closer these are related to the child's own 'natural' concerns, the better.

But what does this amount to? If we consider an example outside the moral area, such as the learning of mathematics or history, it is at once obvious that the child cannot learn anything at all except by stepping *outside* and *beyond* his 'natural' experience. We may, perhaps for good psychological reasons, wish to start with 'real-life' situations: the child may be interested in the number of children in his class, or in what his grandmother did when she was a girl. We may *use* these to develop his thinking in the fields of mathematics and history. But such development cannot occur unless the child is encouraged to drop, or at least go beyond, his immediate 'real-life' concerns, and grasp facts and concepts which are *not* part of those concerns – concepts about addition and subtraction, the measurement of time by centuries, and all that goes to make up what we mean by 'mathematics' and 'history'.

So too with morality. If we consider awareness of others' feelings (EMP), for instance, it is apparent that we shall need to make use *both* of 'real-life' contexts *and* of more 'academic' or 'abstract' learning-situations. We use the pupil's immediate experiences – what he thinks his father or class-mate is feeling, whether he believes that teacher is cross with him, and so on – *in order to* encourage him to go beyond them and improve his EMP generally. We teach him, perhaps, about the various emotions *in general* – their characteristic symptoms, facial expressions, etc. – by using examples and by other methods, so that he can develop an ability which he can then bring to bear on his practical living. We cannot say *a priori* how much we need 'real-life' contexts and how much we need 'academic' contexts: this will depend on the pupil, as well as on the merits of particular methods.

3. A further claim is that the '*social mix*' or clientele of the school is sufficient, or at least necessary, to do much of the work of the moral educator for him. In one common contemporary form, the claim is that by merely mixing different pupils, of different ability and different social class, we shall achieve a more 'democratic', or 'egalitarian', or 'tolerant', or 'concerned' school society. (In our terms,

the pupils will develop more PHIL). By contrast (it is said), to segregate ability-groups or social classes is bound to produce a more intolerant and prejudiced attitude, just as the segregation of white and black produces race prejudice.

However, not only is there no empirical evidence for this, but it is *a priori* highly unlikely that the 'social mix' theory puts its finger on the main point. At a (nameless) international school, an interviewer said to the children of one (nameless) country: 'I suppose mixing with all these different races and nationalities must make you understand and like them more? I expect it's opened your eyes, hasn't it?' The children said words to the effect: 'It certainly has. Before, in our country, we used to quite like the —ians and the —ish: they were different from us, but fun to be with sometimes. But now we have to mix with them every day – well, they're awful. I shan't want to live near them when I grow up'. And so said all the other racial groups.

Equally (one might add) it is not clear that the *amount of mixing* between, say, men and women, or old people and young people, produces more tolerance, concern, or liking. (It is tempting to argue the opposite.) The point here, however, is not to frame hypotheses, but to see that teaching PHIL is *by its nature* more complex than such doctrinaire hypotheses allow. The amount of mixing, whatever it is to be, is plainly relevant: but it can do no more than make *possible* the learning of PHIL. For to have PHIL is not just to 'get used to' the existence of others who are of a different colour, or I.Q., or social class, or age, or hair-style, from oneself: nor even to 'understand' such others. PHIL involves understanding the *reasons for which* the other's needs and wants count equally with one's own. And this is not something which 'social mix', even in principle, can achieve.

This last example in particular will, I hope, show something of the complexity of the relationship between the 'academic' and 'social' contexts of learning. But there is still one more doctrinaire hurdle to surmount. Many people, who will already have appreciated the general points made above, may be inclined to react by saying something like: 'Yes, we understand all this. We understand that neither purely "academic" contexts nor purely "social" contexts are enough. We understand that we must not be wedded to particular models of moral learning, nor expect direct results merely by making changes in one particular direction. We need *both* "academic" *and* "social" contexts'.

All this is true; but it is not enough. For it is apt to lead to (or incorporate) the idea that the two types of context can be *dissociated* from each other. Thus, to take an extreme example, one might imagine a headmaster saying: 'Right, we need both academic and social contexts. Very well, we can fix the academic ones O.K.: we will have classroom periods about emotions, and politics and economics, and moral values. Now how about the social contexts? Well, people speak highly about the Outward Bound courses, school cruises, various kinds of summer camps, and so on: I must arrange for my pupils to be sent on these. Then they will have had both kinds of moral learning.'

This is a silly (though, I think, not uncommon) way of dealing with the problem, because we can see what is likely to happen. The pupils will learn something in their 'academic' contexts, but it is unlikely to transfer to their actual behaviour: conversely, they will acquire certain behaviour-patterns (perhaps in a sense 'learn') from climbing mountains or going on canoe-trips, but if the contexts remain purely 'social' they will not grasp the *reasons* and *principles* required by moral education. Thus I can *both* be taught in a class-room that consideration of other people is morally good, *and* pull my weight in a football-team or on a sailing-ship, and *still* not acquire a generalized principle of PHIL which will affect my behaviour on land or off the games-field. In the former context the reasons are 'unreal', not connected with my experience: in the latter there may be no reasons given at all, or the reasons may be the wrong ones (to win the game or keep the ship afloat).

This leads to the first of three more positive points I want to make about the subject of this section:

(a) CROSS-REFERENCES FROM 'ACADEMIC' TO 'SOCIAL'
What we have to have in mind, whenever we are thinking generally about 'methods of moral education', is a picture of a *range* of different methods which can be placed for convenience on a dimension labelled 'real-life' at one end and 'theoretical' on the other. Thus, getting pupils to cooperate on some 'real-life' task such as sailing a ship would stand at one extreme: explaining to them the ('abstract' or 'philosophical' but very important) reasons why one ought to be concerned about others' interests at the other.

But as we have seen, this is not enough. We have to make sure that the range of different methods, and the different contexts which they require, are *connected*. By 'connected' we must mean, not necessarily that they are given to the same children, or run by the same teacher, or occur during the same school term or year. We must mean that the same *point*, the same *things learned*, become clear to the pupils in *all* the contexts. In order to ensure this, we have to have a very clear idea ourselves of which things they are actually supposed to be learning: and we also have to arrange our methods so that this becomes as clear to the pupils as it should be to us.

Both these are more difficult than they might seem. To use our previous example, suppose we conceive the 'sailing-ship' experience as a matter of 'encouraging self-reliance and responsibility', 'getting pupils to work together', etc.: and suppose we add to this an academic context in which we tell them the parable of the Good Samaritan, point out the virtues of loving one's neighbour, and so on. Now here our *own* picture of the point of the two contexts is confused: they have no real connection in our minds, except in the vaguest possible terms. If, on the other hand, we described the point of the 'sailing-ship' context in terms of 'getting pupils to experience and appreciate the value and equality of other human beings', claiming perhaps that this 'value and equality' becomes clearer to pupils in this sort of 'real-life' context – then we should already have brought the point nearer to the (same) point of the academic 'Good Samaritan' context.

In order to get clear pictures of the points of various contexts, I can only recommend that the teacher gains as firm a grasp as possible of the moral components. A proper understanding of what PHIL, EMP, etc. *mean* is the only thing that will arm him against muddle – not just philosophical muddle, but the practical muddle and in-effectiveness that arises from the lack of clear objectives in choosing contexts. This point stands, even if empirical research eventually shows that certain contexts 'work', in the sense of increasing certain components. For it will be necessary for their 'working' that the teacher, who controls the contexts, understands what he is trying to do. It is not the ropes and the sails, or the opening of Bibles, or any other environmental feature in itself that does the trick: it is the way in which the teacher encourages the children to learn from these features and what they generate.

Even when the teacher is clear, it is essential that he makes the children equally clear. This can only be done by what I have called 'cross-references' from one context to another. By this I mean that ways must be found of getting the pupils to *put together* the various contexts. For example, we do not *just* put them in a sailing-ship and let 'life teach them': we discuss the experience while they are on the ship, take films and tape-recordings of how they behave, consider what general principles emerge, etc. We do not just tell them to love their neighbours: we use examples, illustrations from books, films, and real life: we get them to role-play and act such illustrations for themselves, engage in simulation-situations, and take part in 'real-life' contexts (back to the sailing-ship).

Cross-referencing will enable us to use contexts which affect the development of all the components: and if we use contexts throughout the whole range, along the 'theoretical' – 'real-life' dimension, we shall be saved from many fruitless worries about whether any *one* context does the job – the answer being that of course it does not, but that it will help to do this job in conjunction with other contexts. To take a simple example, suppose we use 'old people' as a topic-title for part of our moral education. Then we can get the children to learn the 'hard' facts about the conditions under which old people live (GIG), to understand why they are just as important as anyone else (PHIL), to develop understanding of how old people feel (EMP), and connected with all this to make decisions (KRAT(1)) and take action (KRAT(2)) by going out to help them, talking to them, and so on: bringing back these experiences to the more 'academic' contexts in which GIG, EMP and PHIL may be further developed, and then going back to the 'real-life' context again by (say) asking some of them to tea, or inviting them to help in the school, or whatever.

It is already clear – and this is what we shall be concerned with for most of what follows in this Part – that in order to do this we have to have 'social arrangements' in the school (an organizational structure) which make it possible. For the classroom or 'academic' context is plainly insufficient for some of the methods we will want to deploy. This leads on to our next point.

(b) MAKING THE SOCIAL CONTEXT FIT THE METHODS

Having a clear picture of *what* we want the pupils to learn is more than half the battle: and having a clear idea of what *methods*, in general, will be effective is most of the other half. From this most of our practical decisions about what changes in the social and organizational arrangements of the school will follow.

I stress this point because it is very easy to regard social contexts as *in themselves* 'educational', or on other grounds desirable. Much of our thinking here tends to be dominated by tradition, fashion, or

administrative convenience. It is one or other of these three temp-
ters, rather than any serious reflection on our own part, which is
probably responsible for most of the social features and arrangements of schools. It is (or is not) traditional for pupils to wear
uniform: fashion changes, and the school caps come off. 'Houses' in
a school may exist because they have always existed in that school:
or because it is administratively convenient to divide pupils up in
this way: or because it is fashionable to do so. 'Morning assembly'
may be retained because it is legally required: but because nobody is
clear what the pupils are supposed to learn from it, or what other
benefits are to be derived, we do not know what form to give it.

Similarly it is in terms of current fashion or personal predilection,
rather than in terms of moral education, that we incline to think
when we enter arenas entitled 'sixth form colleges', 'the integrated
day', 'team teaching', 'tutor groups', 'comprehensivization', 'the
prefect system', and so forth. Often we are moved by what is popular
with the pupils: sometimes rightly, but not necessarily. Thus we
sometimes fall in with a particular picture of 'the teenager of today'
which, whether true or false, is not judged by any ideal of the
'morally educated person' but rather in the light of what we tend to
regard as iron sociological laws – 'the teenager of today' necessarily
'rebels against authority', 'has his own life-style', 'must be treated
as an adult', 'can't be expected to exercise prefectorial authority',
and so on.

Here too the old, false dichotomy between 'authoritarian' and
'permissive' outlooks lulls us into unreason. We find ourselves
taking sides in an irrational dialectic between 'old-fashioned' or
'progressive' methods: the more 'conservative' or 'right-wing' of us
will want to stick to certain traditions and styles, the more 'liberal'
or 'left-wing' will be carried away by the images of 'participation',
'freedom' and many others. We find ourselves fighting battles which
rapidly become political rather than educational. All this is extremely
tedious: but it is also extremely widespread, particularly in current
educational literature, and it needs to be resisted.

All that we have to do (but it is a lot) is to be clear in our own
minds that whatever social arrangements we make *have point*, and that
this point derives from a clearly-stated educational task. The crucial
thing is the *logical* derivation of one from the other. For instance, it
is useless to argue on general grounds about whether pupils should
be encouraged to talk in class, or whether we should have desks in
rows or chairs in a circle: there is absolutely no point in defending or

attacking these arrangements as 'good for participation', 'bad for discipline', 'democratic', etc. The question is, what are we trying to *do* in making these arrangements? Well, if what we are trying to do is to teach discussion-skills – to give pupils practice in the role of discussing and arguing as equals, listening to each other, making relevant replies, and so on – then it will more or less follow logically that they must be encouraged to talk, and that putting the chairs in a circle is a good idea. On the other hand, if what we are trying to do is to give the pupils some information, as quickly and efficiently as possible, then they will not be encouraged to talk, and the arrangement of desks in rows in front of the teacher is probably a sensible one.

This example is (deliberately) naïve. But apply this now to 'social arrangements' in a fuller sense. We can see that 'discussion as equals' entails certain contexts and rules: but what lies behind such important arrangements as the house system, the tutor group, the desire (or refusal) to set and stream, the merits (demerits) of coeducation and a 'charismatic' headmaster, school outings, organized games, and so forth? We cannot just accept them as *given :* but what are the basic educational points from which they are supposed to flow?

In the case of highly functional institutions, such as an army or a sailing-ship, the point of social arrangements is usually fairly obvious: they are required by the function of the institution. In order to fight well, or keep the ship off the rocks, large numbers of (non-disputable) rules and requirements are needed. But part, at least, of the function of the school is educational: and this makes clarity much more difficult. If we were setting out to produce good stormtroopers, or good monks, or good army officers, it would be easier: but this is training or indoctrination, not education. We are trying to produce good *people*. And unless we stick very closely to the moral components, taking our methods from what we guess to be relevant to their development, we shall not get very far.

(c) PRECONDITIONS FOR EDUCATION
In Section A we drew a sharp distinction between educational and other objectives, connecting 'educational' specifically with the development of awareness and rationality – with *learning*. The distinction is important, for we have to be clear about our *aims*. But it does not imply that everything which we arrange in the school must, in itself, be a process of learning or the development of rationality. This is particularly relevant to the social arrangements

which we shall be discussing in later sections and it is important to be clear about it.

If a child is miserable and in pain, it is obviously not much good trying to teach him anything (educate him). So, we send for the doctor, and try to cheer him up. We do not, however, say 'Oh, good, now he's happy again, we've done our job': that would be to forswear any interest in education. What we say is 'Good, now we can *teach* him something'. As educators, we do not look on the child's happiness or freedom from pain as ends in themselves: we regard them only as *preconditions* for education.

The educator is interested solely in how much learning (education) he can generate. He is not a doctor, or a clinical psychiatrist, or a food-provider, or a merchant of happiness. But he will, of course, recognize that unless certain preconditions are established, he simply has no chance of effectively educating. We must beware here, too, of doctrinaire views. It is equally absurd to say (a) that the child's happiness and security make *no* difference to how well we can educate him, or (b) that unhappy and insecure children cannot learn effectively. (a) was, perhaps, fashionable a century ago: (b) is becoming fashionable today. Both are plainly false. We have to compromise. But the *criterion* of whatever compromise we make, as educators, is simply whether this or that arrangement will generate the most education.

Now I shall want to argue, in later sections, that there are certain very important types of learning which cannot occur without a proper 'social base': that is, without the pupil being initiated into a kind of life (a 'tradition', if you like) which makes certain psychological or social phenomena possible. I shall argue, for instance, that there are some things he will not be able to learn unless he has a fairly strong emotional relationship with an adult teacher, or a strong 'group-identity' with his peers. The point I want to make here (which is independent of the merits of any specific later suggestions) is that we must avoid two mistakes. (1) We must not say 'Having a strong emotional relationship with the teacher, etc. is *in itself* educationally valuable': for plainly it is not – it might be used in such a way that the pupil ends up disastrously. (2) Neither must we say 'Having a strong emotional relationship, etc. may be useless for education (since it isn't a process of *learning* anything), but it is important for the pupil's happiness, mental health, etc.'. What we have to say is (3) 'Having a strong emotional relationship, etc. is a *necessary precondition* for education in this area'.

It does not much matter whether or not the reader agrees with the particular suggestion here made. Whatever social arrangements he makes will not go too far wrong so long as he puts (3) into the form of an initial question: 'Is x or y a necessary precondition for education?', and uses his imagination, intelligence and experience to get an answer. He will be able also, of course, to draw on the general findings of psychology and the social sciences, as I have done: indeed, if he asks the question with sufficient earnestness, he can hardly help being compelled to take a hard look at clinical and developmental psychology. But the most important thing is to ask the question.

C. THE FAMILY MODEL

What is wrong with the social set-up of schools as we have it? When asked this, teachers are apt to say such things as (I quote here from informal tape-recordings): 'It doesn't give you a chance to really know your pupils', 'The examination system doesn't give us time to treat our pupils as people', 'We keep having the parents complain', 'You have to change classes all the time, everybody runs around like mad things', 'It's a nine-to-four academic factory, not a school at all', 'The headmaster is just an administrator, the boys hardly know who he is'. All these comments are to the point. Can we generalize them in such a way that we can use the generalizations to determine practical changes?

Some of the comments point to practical pressures (e.g. of examinations) which could in principle be removed, or handled by other methods: these we shall deal with later. Apart from these, the burden of the complaint is simple: it is that the social arrangements of the school *do not give scope for personal relationships*. More precisely, for of course it is not being said that pupils cannot make friends at school, they do not give scope for the kind of relationships required for moral education: perhaps particularly for interaction between staff and pupils. There is no *social base* for this: that is, no *place* and no *contexts of activity* which would naturally generate this interaction. Of course we are here overstating the case: most schools have *some* sort of 'social base', even if it is only morning assembly or the playground. But the lack is felt.

With what can we associate this lack of 'social base?' Elsewhere[1] I jotted down a number of points, at once vague and obvious, which

[1] *I.M.E.*, p. 405.

seemed to be required in any serious attempt to 'morally educate' pupils. They included:

1. The pupil's need for a secure framework in terms of a group-identity.
2. His need for a 'personal identity' in terms of feeling confident, successful, useful and wanted.
3. The importance of close personal contact with adults.
4. The importance of parent-figures and of a firm and clearly-defined authority.
5. The need to channel and institutionalize aggression.
6. The importance of cooperation as against competition.
7. The importance of getting the pupil to participate.

And so forth. Nobody, I imagine, will want to say 'No' to any of these: they are boringly truistic. Yet it should strike us that, not only in schools but also in institutions of higher education, we simply *do not cater* for these truisms. It is not clear that we even try very hard to do so: at least, individuals may try, but there is not much sign of collective effort.

What could we conceivably use as a 'model' situation which *does* take care of these obvious needs? Some readers will at once think of the traditional pattern of the 'public' independent boarding-schools: and this model is indeed relevant. But I shall not make use of it here, because the key points lie deeper. I shall use the model of an even older social institution than Winchester College: the family. By this I shall understand a family of reasonable size: say, of four or five children and two parents. The relevance of this model does not, of course, derive from any suggestion that schools should *be* families or that the teacher should replace the parent. It is rather that in the family it appears that certain kinds of needs are catered for, certain kinds of learning-situations naturally set up, and certain elements of the 'social base' we are looking for naturally exist.

Consider this in the light of our seven truisms listed above. In a satisfactory family, the child immediately has a 'group identity' (1): and by being born into it, looked after by his parents, etc. he feels 'wanted' – to which parents will naturally add as much confidence and feeling of success as they can (2). He is *eo ipso* in close personal contact with adults (3), and authority is clearly defined by the parents (4). Not all families solve their children's aggression-problems (5), but there is a built-in necessity for a good deal of cooperation which will mitigate them to some extent, at least until adolescence (6). Finally, the child cannot help but 'participate' (7).

What is it that holds families together, and what is it that provides the 'social base' for the immense amount of learning that the child does in the family? How is it that he learns to talk and argue, to behave cleanly, to control his impulses ,to master all the many facts and skills that he learns outside school? We do not have to be expert social psychologists to give a general answer to this question. First, the family lives in one place, and has forms of sharing which bind it together. Not only are they an economic unit, but they share food, drink, holidays, outings and in general all the aspects of life which fall outside the area of work. (Though even some forms of work – and this is important – may be shared, such as housework which the childs helps with, minor jobs in which he helps his father or elder brothers, and so on.) Secondly, the child has a strong *emotional* relationship with his parents (and siblings). From father and mother will come approval and disapproval, love, anger, and all the other emotions: and the child will reflect them back to the same sources. He will learn in order to please, or be like, father or brother, to help mother, to be rewarded by sister, even to commend himself to aunt or grandparent. These people *count* with him: they are all he has.

All this too is obvious enough: and it ought to be equally obvious that too few educational institutions (particularly from the secondary school onward) have made any serious attempt to introduce these factors into their social systems. It has been assumed (tacitly) that the school exists only, or chiefly, to impart information; and that parents or 'society' will do the rest. Clearly this assumption is insane; but it needs to be seen why this is so. For it is emphatically *not* just a matter of schools having to 'fill the gap' which has been created by 'bad homes', or the difficulties of bringing up children in an urban and industrialized society. The whole picture painted in terms of parents doing all the moral education, and the school being required only to pass on knowledge and culture, is a false one: and it would be false even if the 'nuclear' or otherwise unsatisfactory families of today were to be replaced by 'better' families (an unlikely prediction in itself).

There are two points here. First, there *is* no other way whereby the child can learn, or will want to learn, except the way in which he learns in the family: that is, with a secure 'social base', close contact with adults, and so forth. This is a necessary model simply because it is the *child's* model, and the only one he has. To expect efficient learning without a base at all, or on some quite different base, is just silly. (Yet this is what we seem to expect by putting children behind desks from nine to four, and trying to persuade them to learn things.) Secondly, the picture is insane because it implies a sharp break between two different situations: (a) the situation in which the child (or teenager) is in his own family, under parental authority and protection, and (b) the situation in which he is expected to be responsible for himself, which involves financial independence and perhaps the additional role of husband/wife and father/mother. The implication is that the child can move from the one to the other, from (a) to (b), without difficulty or training. No room is left for any intermediary community between (a) and (b).

It is worth pointing to some of the more obvious symptoms of our failure to cater for these simple truths. Perhaps the most obvious is the existence of teenage or sub-teenage groups and gangs which are not under any kind of educational control, and whose emotional investment is anywhere but in the school or college. With this go many symptoms of the 'youth culture': some upsetting, like drug-taking, others less so, like fashions in clothes and music. Again, teachers do not need to be told of the resistance, the 'uphill' nature of the task of teaching many pupils: they simply do not want to learn – and one has the horrid suspicion that new curricular methods alone (team-teaching, 'progressive' methods, visual aids, 'real-life' projects and so on) will not do the trick: the teacher may work himself into the ground trying to amuse and educate the pupils, but the motivation is just not there. They don't care.

And (one might add) why should they? If – as is sometimes the case – we take little personal interest in them, they will take little in us. Apart from such interest, where is their motivation to come from? Not, or not much, from the intrinsic fascination of a still largely academic curriculum. Not even from the more 'interesting' and 'real life' subjects – for in fact the pupil's position is still intensely artificial and *un*real. Disguise it how we may, the school (as we have it) is an institution for learning, not for amusement or for having a good time: and why should they learn if they have no emotional investment in the place? A little, perhaps, in order to get on – to get better jobs, a place at the university, a chance for higher standards of living. But to expect healthy children and adolescents to spend most of their time sitting down and learning school subjects (however delightfully presented) *without* very strong emotional incentive seems to me grotesquely naïve. No doubt they will, for the most part, go through the motions; but not much more than that.

One fashionable reaction to this is tacitly to abandon the notion of education and any serious learning in favour of other notions. We recognize that many, perhaps most, children are not suited to an 'academic approach': very well, let us rather be content to encourage 'creativity', 'self-expression', 'everyday knowledge', 'social aware-ness' and so forth. Let there be dance, drama, woodwork: let light and colour abound in schools, and let the walls be covered with (bad) paintings by the pupils: let them at all costs *do* something, even if they learn nothing. Let the success of our new methods be judged by pupil-interest and pupil-popularity, by the amount of activity that goes on: not, please, by any assessment which is concerned with judging how much they actually know, or how much progress they have made towards rationality in the various 'forms of thought' described by educational philosophers.[1]

I do not intend this as pure parody; many of the practices advocated may be educationally desirable. But it seems plain that the reason why they are advocated is the existing (or previous) lack of *motivation* in many children. Faced with sullen teenagers sitting in grim rows, or bored eight-year-olds struggling with English grammar, one might well want to try anything which will engage their interest. It is not clear to me why the 'intrinsic' motivation of interest in a subject is always and everywhere to be preferred to the 'extrinsic' motivation of strict discipline, and (if necessary) fear. But in any case the point is missed. We shall not get enough, or the right sort of motivation unless we set up a system which is sufficiently *like* that of the family to generate the required emotions.

I am saying nothing very original here, in that there are and have been schools where *some* of the relevant features of the family have been set up. Apart from occasional 'progressive' schools, however, such as A. S. Neill's and others, most of such schools are identified with a particular 'public school' tradition. It is worth pointing out that this tradition (for which I have considerable admiration, and on which I shall draw heavily) does not seem to have been founded on the family model: or if it has, then the model seems to be that of the patriarchal, emotionally repressed, and single-sex (if this makes sense) family. This may serve as a convenient example of the importance of the *general* model.

For instance, the absence of significant mother-figures in single-sex schools (despite house matrons and masters' wives) is perhaps more important, in terms of the family model, than the absence of

[1] See Hirst and Peters, *The Logic of Education*.

co-pupils of the opposite sex – about which there is a good deal of fuss, and to remedy which sporadic attempts are made by fashionable headmasters. For the child's relationship with his mother will inevitably be important, not just because of his future sex life, but because it will affect his motivation for learning. The point is not, as some critics would like to claim, that 'homosexuality is encouraged':[1] nor even that boarding-school males are 'bad at getting on with women'.[2] It is rather that one whole important area of the child's development and learning-capacity is simply left out.

Again, criticisms of the boarding-schools as 'artificial', 'total institutions', 'indoctrinating with rigidly-enforced norms', etc. sometimes miss the point. For *our* point, at least, is not at all that such institutions are 'too much' of a community, so to speak – not that the child is put into a highly 'potent' community which only *too* successfully reproduces the family setting, whereas the child ought to be left to his own devices. It is rather that the institution does not *sufficiently* reproduce the family; and it is largely in failing to do this that the features to which critics object are still too often preserved. There is, as there should be, strong emotional investment in the community: there is 'team spirit', hard work, loyalty, personal attention, supervision of boys by older boys (cf. the role of elder brothers in a family), the 'binding rituals' of communal eating and communal enterprises. All this (in the proper forms) is excellent. But where, we might say, are the other features of the normal family – the running to mother in tears, the problems with girl friends, the natural expressions of emotion and mood?

My intention here is neither to criticize nor praise the boarding-school tradition: only to show that anyone would be a fool not to take it seriously as a quarry or source of information for those seeking important elements for a 'social base'; and that nevertheless it would be a methodological mistake to start with this tradition and try to fill in its gaps. We need to get a clearer idea of the psychological and sociological roots of the sort of community which can be educationally effective: hence the family model.

There is one respect in which the model, at least as instanced by the modern urban family, is seriously inadequate. This is the difficulty of making the parents' work-situation real to the child.

[1] To prove this would require careful control-groups: in any case the merits of latent as against overt homosexuality are not clear to me.

[2] There is no evidence for this either: anyway, what is to count as 'getting on with'? (Some critics seem to mean 'getting off with'.)

Suppose, by contrast, that we are dealing with a child on a frontier farm. The parents are both, in an important sense, 'at home': mother does the housework, cooks, minds the children: father looks after the farm. Johnny and Molly can tag along with either of them, helping (or hindering) both father and mother. They are part of a 'real' situation: 'real', in the sense that even the dullest Johnny and Molly can see that if the cows escape or the dishes are broken genuine misfortune occurs. It is not something that they are merely *told about* by parents or teachers. They are aware of constant 'pay-off', both nice and nasty, as a result of their own and their parents' and siblings' behaviour in a non-artificial world.

In the urban community, however, father goes out to work at some nameless and (to the child) unintelligible job in an office: mother may work also, and if she stays at home she is likely to cut her role as housekeeper and child-rearer down to a minimum, thus making it non-imitable to the child. The child is surrounded, at no great distance, with a complex economy which he may never understand, though he may grow to resent its operations when he becomes adolescent: and there will be every kind of impulse-attraction in the form of toys, bright lights, films, TV, and other things designed for consumption rather than use. He may change homes frequently: the family may not, unless it makes a special effort, engage in many cooperative activities at all: and his interaction with the immediate city-folk is likely to be in terms of their social roles rather than with them as people.

All this we complain about already, under various headings: we could perhaps regard it as a regrettable falling-away of the family from what we still conceive (and are nostalgic about) as its 'proper role'. We do not have to sentimentalize about the Victorian family singing hymns round the harmonium, or the spacious if primitive age of the family in 'frontier' cultures such as the Wild West, in order to have a fairly clear idea of this 'proper role'. Nor do we have to connect it necessarily with particular codes of morality. We have only to appreciate the force of its *format*, the structure of the 'social base' which it gives. If the crucial features are to be found in exceptional family- or group-structures, such as some of the Israeli kibbutzim, I have no quarrel: I pick the traditional family because it is more familiar (the pun is significant), and because I have doubts about attempted replacements.

It will be said, rightly, that some schools (perhaps primary schools in particular) are already moving towards this model. It will also be said that the model plainly requires considerable alteration if it is to apply to older teenagers and students in higher education. Both these points are worth noting: but my purpose here has been merely to present the model and some of its basic features, so that we can see what is missing from standard school practice.

D. Requirements for the School (1)

In what follows I shall stick my neck out and simply suggest, without benefit of lengthy psychological argument, what seems to me to be required if the school is to have social arrangements effective for moral education. The reader should remember:

(i) Practical difficulties in actually making such arrangements will be considered in a later section: the reader must at this stage prevent himself from the reaction 'Yes, that's all very well, but it's not *practical*, we can't *do* it'. We first need a clear picture of what we *want* to do (and, as I hope to show, I shall not in fact make many impractical suggestions).

(ii) Equally we shall postpone consideration of how these suggestions tie in with other (non-moral) forms of education – another ground on which some of them might be thought 'impractical'.

(iii) I shall be tailoring these suggestions to fit the secondary school: that is, roughly, any school whose pupils begin at any age after 11 years, continuing to any age from about 15 to 20. Their relevance to other educational institutions, however, should not be too obscure.

(a) DECENTRALIZATION AND THE 'HOUSE'

I consider here the most important, and also the most obvious, requirement which the family model seems to imply. If schools are to operate in any serious respect like the family, and to generate the conditions of learning and the 'social base' which the family so well deploys, it is clear that there must be some decentralization. I shall speak of this in terms of the 'house', in the hope that the word will be familiar (but not tendentious) in this context.

The answer to the question 'What makes a house?' will be in many respects similar to the question 'What makes a family?': and there will be parallels to other questions and answers, such as 'What makes a good housemaster (father)?' or 'good prefect (elder brother)?' Obviously enough, simply to *call* one group of pupils 'X House' because their names come in the first half of the alphabet, and another group 'Y House' because their names come in the last half, is unsatisfactory. What do we need to add? Will it help if they parade as houses for an occasional fire practice? Not much, we might think. Very well, then, what will? I suggest the following:

1. *Numbers*
Numbers in a house must not be too large: how small we can make them will depend on manpower. Much over 80 is too large: much under 30 impractical, for most schools. For our purposes we need a community where all the members can know each other pretty well, and be known pretty well by the houseparents (see below). Numbers near the upper end of the scale can be handled, if other arrangements are satisfactory (particularly topographical arrangements: see below).

2. *Composition*
Remember the family. We need all ages (within the secondary school age-range), and both sexes. A house composed 'horizontally', i.e. of pupils of the same age-range or the same academic attainment, is not a family-type house at all, but a vaguely institutionalized peer-group or club. It is particularly important (again like the family) that the *older* pupils should play a full part.

3. *Houseparents*
In charge of the house there will naturally be both a housemaster and a housemistress, representing father and mother. I need not add that they will be chosen, and trained, for 'parental' or pastoral ability, rather than for academic qualifications. Most of their time and energy will be devoted to the house. Their prestige and power in the school must be high.

4. *Locale and topography*
Families have homes. One thing that makes a home is shared space: another is individuality. It must be possible for members of the house to engage in normal (non-academic) activities together, in shared space: it must also be possible for them to make it, and feel it as, *their* home/house (which implies both responsibility for it, and independence from outside interference). It must also be 'home-like' in other ways. The topography, furniture, etc. must generate security, 'cosiness', individuality, relaxation. There must be enough privacy, and enough opportunity for sharing.

5. *Shared rituals*
Families keep together by sharing certain rituals and other
activities. In particular, they eat together, drink together, look
after their own homes, and (sometimes) pray together or engage
in some common ceremonial or conventional activity. Houses
must do the same. Some things that families do (e.g. sleep
together) may be impractical for many houses: other things are
simple and quite practical. I stress here what we may call the
'internal' binding-forces in the home/house: they may be less
obvious than its external enterprises and activities, but they are
likely to be even more important.

(b) ACTIVITIES AND SELF-ESTEEM
We do not need professional psychologists to tell us (though they
have done so vociferously) that unless the child feels loved, valued
and wanted he is unlikely to develop well as a person: in particular,
from our point of view, he is unlikely to be able to 'afford' concern
and motivation required to make 'other-considering' moral decisions
(KRAT(I)) and act on them (KRAT (2)). This can be put in various
terms: 'a sense of identity', 'security', 'self-acceptance', 'self-esteem'.
I think we know what we are talking about.
One of the essential preconditions that the 'social base' of the
house will try to generate, then, is this 'self-esteem' for all of its
members. How can this be achieved? I suggest three general
methods:

1. *Multiple criteria of success*
We can approach this negatively by observing that, in a system
where only certain performances are rewarded, only those capable
of such performances are likely to acquire much self-esteem: if
we reward those who do well at work and games, those who are
bad at both will have even less self-esteem than they had before
(which may not have been much). We need, then, to adjust the
'desired performances' and their 'rewards' to the capabilities of
the members of the house, and *not* vice versa. In particular we
need to arrange things so that everyone can shine at something,
however stupid, clumsy or otherwise incompetent he may be.
To take an example: suppose (if this is not too unfashionable
for modern ears) that we arrange to have an inter-house cup or
prize. We allow houses to tot up points for various activities –
winning the football matches, passing examinations, or whatever.

Now we so select the activities that it is not only the competent performers – the star athletes or scholars – who can score the points for their house. We add the possibility of scoring points for music, or mending motor-bikes, or mackerel-fishing. We so organize it that the performance of the 2nd or 3rd house football team counts for as much as the performance of the 1st team. We stop only when we are reasonably assured that everyone can contribute *something*.

'Success' depends on the 'rewards' given, in this context. Of course these can be of any form, from material rewards to the mere approbation of the housemaster, via the prestige traditionally attached by the house to certain activities. Simple institutionalized forms, like the house competition mentioned above, are only useful ways of attaching prestige and rewards to new performances.

2. *Cooperative activities (external and internal)*
The pupil will naturally want to shine at something: if possible, to do something better than anyone else. We must not try (vainly) to abolish this by any doctrinaire view about the merits of 'cooperation against competition'. But of course it will be true that, however hard we juggle our rewards, there will be some pupils who are to be classified as failures in terms of individual performance. However, there are two other ways in which the house can do something about this.

The first is by external cooperative activities: that is, activities which depend on collective effort to achieve some external goal. Organized games are the classic example: others are, for instance, building something; putting on a play or a concert; running a farm or a business. I do not need to say any more about these: they are standard practice, even if not incorporated into a proper house system.

The second requires more consideration. By 'internal' cooperative activities I mean activities which have no external goal (to win the game, make the business pay), but are overtly devoted to cooperation and mutual assistance. For example: getting older pupils to help the younger with their work and other things: having sessions in which the object is to encourage or help unhappy members, 'misfits', or those who are generally a nuisance in the house: allowing the pupils to make and administer their own rules and discipline. (Unfashionable institutions such as 'fagging' may take on a more favourable appearance in this light; the various ways in which some members of the house can be *of use* to others are all valuable here.)

3. *Opportunities to 'patronize'*
Characteristically in schools pupils are on the receiving end. They are *done things to* or *at :* they are always in a subordinate role. This does not encourage self-esteem. The pupil must, sometimes, be in a position to feel superior: to patronize, protect, teach, command, and control.

This can be achieved by various methods, e.g.: (i) making sure all members have *dependants*, whether in the form of younger children, animals, individuals outside the house or school whom they can protect and help (infants, backward children, old people, etc.): (ii) making sure that each member is allowed to cash in on his possession of particular skills or talents, by teaching them to others (including older members and adults) and thereby temporarily assuming an 'authority' role: (iii) in real-life or simulation situations, actually giving the junior members powers, responsibilities and authority. (They run the house for a week, for example: or control the house finances, or conduct the rituals, or organize its activities.)

4. *Physical warmth*
To some extent it is true that self-esteem arises because of successful performance, because of taking part in cooperative activities, and because of being able to 'patronize': these we have tried to take care of in 1, 2 and 3 above respectively. But this will not be enough. Again, it requires no professional psychologist to tell us that the confidence that goes with 'feeling wanted' or 'being loved' has a great deal to do with simple physical experiences.

Very important for the young child, we are told both by psychologists and by ordinary mothers and fathers, are the straightforward physical expressions of love – cuddling, touching, and other forms of bodily contact: the warmth and communication of shared unsophisticated physical activity. To suppose that the child will have totally outgrown the need for this when he reaches the secondary-school age is just silly. Indeed it is apparent, from the kind of quasi-sexual communal 'clinging' that is characteristic of many adolescents, that they have not grown out of it even in the late teens – perhaps because they have not had enough of it earlier.

Some will think of sex in this context, and we shall take a look at this later.[1] But we are not talking about the specifically sexual (whatever that is). I have in mind then natural physical contexts, recreative and reassuring for all people, of (say) engaging in a sort of mass free-for-all in the swimming-pool, some forms of dancing, some cooperative gymnastic activities. These go together with the encouragement of overt person-to-person physical expression. The importance of this is, of course, *felt* (more or less consciously) even in the most 'stiff upper lip' schools: its repression is part of a tradition we have to get rid of. This does not mean, in case anyone is frightened, that there may not be natural or inevitable desires for physical privacy among pupils of all ages, which have to be respected: but to advocate the expression of sympathy, comradeship, etc. by overt physical means is not to advocate force or interference. The complexities of our existing tradition are such that, besides encouraging social or institutional forms, we shall probably need open discussions and other more 'direct' methods as well.

(c) COLLECTIVE RESPONSIBILITY AND 'PAY-OFF'
Our third major heading indicates quite a different way in which the decentralized house described in (a) above can operate. On the one hand, it must give its members confidence and self-esteem ((b) above): but on the other hand, it must not attempt to shield them from the world as it is. Indeed, it must bring them face-to-face with the laws (both natural and social) of that world in as crisp a manner as possible. This is perhaps an area where changes in school practice are most of all required.

I can best illustrate the main point here by an example; and I shall take one of the toughest examples from the point of view of the practising teacher, the example of drug-taking. It will be well known to teachers who have any considerable experience in this area that very little can be achieved by just *talking* to the children and teenagers who take drugs, and not much more by doing our best to ensure that they do not get their hands on drugs. We can point out to them the consequences, admonish them, threaten them with the law, and so forth – a large number will just not care. So what do we do? Well, one thing we do is to send them for special psychiatric attention, or put them in specially-organized communities for the cure of drug-addicts, or support and sustain them

[1] See p. 131.

in various ways. And of course this is not totally silly, because no doubt drug-takers have psychological problems which need attention. But there is an important sense in which it is artificial. Why (we might begin by asking) should people not take drugs? One obvious reason is that it reduces their ability to perform their obligations to other people. The practicability of taking drugs in a society constantly threatened by external enemies, for instance, would be minimal: if you are an ancient Roman surrounded by barbarians, both the task itself and the other ancient Romans would make sure that you are able to stand to arms whenever required, rather than lying in a stupor. Questions about the 'personal morality' or 'ideal' of drug-taking (as contrasted with our wicked materialist society, for instance) just would not arise. It is our misfortune – or rather, our fault – that we have a society in which drug-takers can get away with it.

If this *is* at least *one* good reason for not taking drugs, then the educator has to instantiate this reason in a social context; and a purely academic context is unlikely to be sufficient. (Pupils in drugged stupors are sometimes difficult to distinguish from pupils in ordinary stupors.) The question therefore becomes: under what sort of conditions will it become obvious to the members of the house that drug-taking is just plain *inconsistent* with what the world requires? Showing that drug-taking is inconsistent with working hard, or being good at football, is not crisp enough: we have to do more. Very well: we put the house into situations where, if people take drugs, they get savaged by their peers because they have not pulled their weight in gathering food: or they get left behind in a stupor on the cold mountain-side: or they are given no food because they have failed to wash up: or, if absolutely necessary, they run the risk of being eaten by wolves.

I have deliberately overstated this, to make the point. The point is that both school and society are, from the child's viewpoint, so artificial and remote from the underlying realities of life that the lessons need to be driven home in as simple and strong a fashion as possible. This, of course, is the attraction of what we may call the 'Outward Bound' school of thought: on mountains or in sailing-ships the necessities of the situation just *are there*, and it requires a very advanced addict, or a very severe degree of 'maladjustment', to avoid them.

To understand, in anything like a full sense, these 'underlying realities' is no easy task for the child. Basic economic facts, like the

necessity to produce food and warmth: basic social facts, like the
necessity to preserve some degree of reputation and credit with one's
neighbours: basic political facts, like the necessity to have some kind
of rules, discipline and sanctions – all these are not made clear to
children (in the way that they would be clear if the child lived in a
smaller, simpler social group). We just assume that children will
somehow pick these truths up: and then we are surprised when, as
adolescents, they show a virtually complete ignorance of them.

Hence the importance of what I have called 'collective responsibility' and 'pay-off'. The former is a matter of the house operating
as a group: if not, the 'pay-off' – the good or bad result – must be
immediate and obvious even to the dullest. Given even a small
number of such experiences, it is to be hoped that the point will
sink in, and can be generalized. Here 'life' has, if you like, taught the
child: the educator's job is to contrive the experiences, and encourage the child to generalize from them. Imagine, for instance, how
much could be learned from a 'Lord of the Flies' situation, carefully
monitored, video-taped, and discussed afterwards: more, one might
guess, than from merely reading the book or seeing the film.

The crux here consists in *putting the members of the house on the
spot:* that is, in giving *them* the responsibility and the consequent
'pay-off'. They run a business or look after their house finances
incompetently: very well, they go broke. They fail to organize food
for themselves: very well, they go hungry. They fail to have adequate
rules about stealing, or punctuality, or telling the truth: very well,
there will be chaos. Of course the houseparents will have to control
this method and keep it within limits: but I am much more scared
that they will not use it strongly enough.

Amongst other things, it is only by bringing them up against the
laws of nature in this way that the 'we-they' feeling is avoidable. In
an artificial situation, the standard peer-group rules about 'not
sneaking' and the barrier between 'we', the pupils, and 'they', the
authorities, is inevitably raised. There is a kind of alienation,
perhaps a 'cold war', between teachers and pupils which is as anti-
educational as it is boring. In a 'real' situation (think of the sailing-
ship again), there is just no scope for the cold war: no time, and not
much incentive.

In this section I have demarcated the three general moves that need
to be made in respect of social arrangements: (a), the establishment

of an effectively-organized and decentralized house – the creation of a social group to work *with*: (b), the task of that group in creating a feeling of security and love for all its members: (c), its task in facing the world we live in and coping with it.

These points, again, are not new: but they need to be institutionalized in our schools. In further sections we shall be looking at some points arising from them, at the practical difficulties, and the first steps to be taken. For the present I would suggest an approach which is as much unlike our usual acceptance of school systems as 'given' as can be imagined, but which is more likely to stimulate creative thinking. Suppose you are a head teacher with 20 other teachers: you are landed on a desert island with about 650 children, and told to educate them, with the help of various buildings and bits of equipment which a mother-country kindly supplies you with. What do you do?

Whatever you do, I bet that (even if you disagree with the specific points made so far) that what you do *not* do is to put them in one collective lump called 'a school', and teach them subjects from 9–1 and again from 2–5 – not even if the school steamer ships them to their parents on neighbouring islands every evening and back again in the morning. What you probably begin by doing is to split them up into manageable groups (houses), which will be able to come to terms with life on the island. You will need to get the groups behind you to make and keep rules (not having the benefit of a police force), and you will no doubt rely on the older members for much of this, and for helping with the groups in general. And so on. At some stage, when you have established an effective 'social base', you will turn your attention towards what the groups can profitably *learn*. Much of the learning, at least in the sphere of moral education, you will find to have taken place already, and to have been firmly appropriated by the pupils: but you will, of course, want to add learning of the various forms of thought and endeavour which (we like to suppose) are at least sometimes incorporated in various 'school subjects'. What you do about this is an open question. But at least you will have got your priorities right.

E. Requirements for the School (2)

I now want to fill in some of the more important gaps left by the last section, where we contented ourselves with looking at three main features in the social arrangements of the school. There are a

E

large number of topics about which I need to say something: they are heterogeneous topics, not neatly classifiable, and they weave in and out of each other and in and out of the three main features. All I can do is to list them in turn: the reader must forgive overlaps and cross-classifications.

I. THE SCHOOL AS A WHOLE

I had better deal with this before anyone asks for their money back ('You entitle one Part "The School Community", and it doesn't deal with the school at all, it just talks about the house system'). Many teachers will be used to regarding the school, or the class (or 'form'), as *the* social unit. But this is not a law of God, and in my view ought not to be a convention of men.

Earlier I have argued in favour of something like the family model, which led us to take the house of about 30–80 pupils as the 'social base' or 'working unit' for moral education. If this is right, almost all schools will be simply too big for our purposes: and the class, though of the right size, is not and cannot be set up like the family. The size of whatever institution we choose to call 'the school' really does not matter, so long as it is properly decentralized into houses as we have described them. The key figures will be the house-master and housemistress.

This does not mean that the school as a whole has *no* function as a 'social base': only that its function is diminished. The headmaster will still be, or can still be, an important figure for moral education; and I should argue strongly in favour of headmasters (or head-mistresses) whose chief abilities lie in the field of exercising authority and pastoral care, selecting and supporting good houseparents, and generally acting as a kind of super-parent (a very useful thing to have around, if you are a housemaster and need some higher authority to refer to). If we want an administrator, somebody to make up the time-table, or a public-relations expert, we can hire one. Similarly the school as a whole will have important functions and activities which will attract the pupils' loyalty and emotional investment, in ways too analogous to those of the house to require lengthy comment: there will be school plays, concerts, football matches, cruises, expeditions, and so forth.

The balance between this and the house activities calls for nice judgement; and the only thing worth saying is that, if in doubt, err on the side of the house. Naturally we do not want totally self-enclosed houses (see under 'Other Groupings' below); but any attempt to detract from the 'potency' of the house as an institution on grounds of economy, administrative convenience or other things that have nothing to do with education should be firmly resisted. The school should act, in a fairly formal way, as an intermediary between the house and the wider society: otherwise it exists for the benefit of the house, and not vice versa.

We are speaking, of course, only about the school's *social* functions. Its *academic* functions are a different matter (we shall deal with these in a later section).[1] But no one need be frightened that the school will lack an important role as an institution of some kind. All that is being said is that it is not the prime institution for moral education via social arrangements.

2. OTHER GROUPINGS AND INDIVIDUALITY

Another fear I may have raised is that of 'regimentation' or 'swallowing up the individual in the house'. First, it needs to be recognized that we are indeed aiming to give the individual pupil the security of a 'group identity'. He must be able to feel himself as 'belonging' to the house, or gang, or group, or the collection of his 'mates', or whatever we call it. In arranging this we create nothing artificial. Fashionably contra-suggestible liberals may pretend that children and teenagers are naturally individualistic, and would remain so were it not for the wicked regimentation of schools, armies, governments and so on. But this cannot be seriously maintained: it is sufficiently obvious that if we do not provide young people with groups, then they form their own. The need to belong is so strong, indeed, that our task may be to get them to grow out of it more quickly than some of them do: but we cannot fulfil that task by pretending that the need is not there. (It is there in adults too, but in a 'detribalised' society we find it hard to satisfy.)

But secondly, of course we must not push this beyond what it will bear. Other groupings must be provided or allowed to form: and individuals must be allowed to be by themselves. Amongst the 'other groupings' we can imagine groupings (i) by age, (ii) by mutual interest, (iii) on the 'social base' of the school as a whole, (iv) by informal contact with the outside world. Time must be made for all this, and for individual privacy, and this is something with which we shall have to experiment.

This affects above all the topography of the house. The ideal system (I do not consider economic practicalities here) is one which

[1] See p. 133 ff.

allows the maximum freedom of choice; it seems foolish to assert loudly that pupils of such-and-such an age 'like to be together' or 'like privacy' – particularly since we do not know, and individual pupils say different things. For instance, imagine a large common-room: about 20 pupils of all ages and both sexes in it: round the walls are tiny cubicles, one per pupil: the door can be open or shut – if shut, with or without a 'do not disturb notice'. The room as a whole is generally controlled by two or three of the older pupils. This topographical arrangement puts participation and privacy at the pupil's disposal: and if I had to decide, this is what I should recommend.[1] One could add topography for other groupings, e.g. a prefects' common-room.

Much is probably gained, though something may also be lost, by siting the school and its houses in not too remote an area. The dangers of 'total institutions', well documented by social scientists, are of course to be watched: and if members of the house spend some of their time in the town outside, this is all to the good. For if we cannot produce a community which keeps them, without force, from spending *all* their time amid the bright lights of pubs and coffee bars and cinemas, we shall have failed anyway. Ideally the school should be sited with 'town' on one side and space on the other, both for convenience and as spatially representing its position as intermediary between the family and the wider society.

Having said this, however, I must warn the reader against the greater temptation of the opposite error. The notion that schools (and universities) must somehow be 'integrated' into 'society' or 'the community' – that it is somehow wickedly unreal or artificial if they are to some degree closed societies – seems to rest on a failure to understand the nature and difficulties of education. (Curiously it is often those who advocate this who also complain loudest about the horrors of modern society.) One of the (many) things we have to teach our pupils is that their values should *not* be those of the wider society: we have to give them an identity *apart* from society, and sometimes by implication in opposition to it. To do this is not to create an enclosed race of snobs: it is simply to have the courage to believe that *educators*, not society, know best what sort of people to produce – and if we do not believe this, then we should not be in business at all. So I do not think the reader should be hesitant about making his house or 'social base' as 'potent' as is necessary to get the job done. The 'potency', the emotional investment in the house,

[1] A close analogy with the 'chamber' system at Winchester College.

can then be *used in relation to* the wider society: but that is another matter (discussed below).

3. EXTERNAL RELATIONS AND INTERNAL 'POTENCY'

The successful building-up of what I have called a 'potent' house or social group may, to begin with, involve getting all its members in a context where they are more or less obliged to act as a group, and temporarily to sever relationships elsewhere: for instance, on a camping holiday, a canoe trip, a mountaineering expedition, or whatever. It is important that this potency, the *integration* of the group, should remain under normal school conditions: and I have suggested means to this end. But the house will also have external relations.

I do not think these relations will prosper unless they are firmly based on a potent house. To put it dramatically, the power, the source of authority, the source of 'goodness', must be the house in the first place: and *from* that base, the *pupils' own* base, various relationships can be set up. On this all else hangs: if we do not establish this, the house becomes a farce or a bore, and our whole opportunity for moral education disappears. So the reader will be careful with his external relationships, until he is sure that the base has been properly set up.

Now consider, for instance, the role of the parent. What should happen here is that the pupils, proud of their intermediary 'home' and its activities, will invite their parents into it. They will act as entertainers (as happens now to some degree with schools as a whole); they will persuade the parents to provide money, furniture, etc. for the house; they will – more important – persuade them to spend *time* in it, helping with (say) the coaching for games, or the art, or drama, or music, or anything. They will be able to initiate their parents *not* just into their purely *academic* achievements, but into a form of life which they, the pupils, have set up for themselves and by themselves (of course with the help of the housemaster: but when the pupils begin to think that they are doing everything, and speak of the housemaster in a tone of benevolent patronage, things are going well).

It is, again, *from* this base that the pupils can issue forth to engage in activities like social service, visiting the sick, the old, etc.: from this that they can ask for money to run some enterprise or expedition, pester parents or governors till they get either a swimming-pool or at least the spades to dig it with: from this that they relate to the shopkeepers, café owners, and other representatives of the outside world, making sure that the house's credit is good, its reputation high, its 'image' satisfactory at least for its own purposes. Given the base, the kind and number of activities which the house can undertake is almost endless. It can (I speak from experience) cope with a small intake of case-hardened juvenile delinquents: build and sail a boat across dangerous seas: look after a small crèche of infants (perhaps more difficult than either): and so forth. We need not worry about the variety of external relations that are possible to such a group.

I will rapidly mention some of the possible 'ordinary' activities which may help to keep a house 'potent', and be in other ways morally educative: each could be considerably expanded, of course:

Holding and administering their own 'house funds'.
Running a small business (farm, garden, etc.).
Entertaining.
Putting on plays, concerts, dances, etc.
Looking after their own bikes, cars, boats, horses, etc.
Games and athletics.
Doing their own repairs and furnishings.
Building, making things.
Doing their own catering, cooking, clothes-mending, washing.
Having their own newspapers, book- and record-library, musical equipment, etc.

All these, in some degree, are practical. The degree depends partly on how clearly the houseparents see the point. For example, if I am the sort of person who thinks it useful for teenage girls to produce beautifully-iced cakes and lobster thermidor under ideal conditions, and allows them to do this in periods jokingly called 'domestic science', then I shall probably not relish the idea of the girl-members of my house hastily cooking a 'scratch' meal every day for themselves and the boy-members. But if I remember that catering is rather more like this than it is like a domestic science class, I shall probably be willing to put up with a good deal of initial chaos and incompetence (until the house forces them to do a bit better). (Compare mothers who keep children out of the kitchen 'because they don't help': no wonder they don't learn.) *Of course*, at least until a respectable tradition is established, this kind of thing will often go wrong and show up the pupils' incompetence: *of course* they are incompetent, because this is probably the first time they have actually been given the responsibility to *run* something. That is the whole point of it.

I am not suggesting that houseparents allow the pupils to be poisoned, or blow themselves up, or run deeply into debt. But I am suggesting that the importance of the 'pay-off' we talked of earlier is such that such mistakes may be the only way of educating. To do it all for them (even if we had the staff) is too easy. I should even be inclined to let a *fair* amount of damage and disaster occur, just to drive the point home. If everyone has stomach-ache because of bad cooking, or somebody breaks an ankle because somebody else has failed to cover up a hole, or the house play gets hissed because they are under-rehearsed, or they go broke because of wild investments in running their business – well, *let it happen*. Then we can start again, and they may be more sensible. A firm grasp of this point will encourage the educator to go far beyond what he may now think to be 'acceptable' in his respectable school and community: perhaps even, with the parents' consent, beyond what the law strictly requires by way of supervision and responsibility for the pupils.

4. ROLES OF THE HOUSEPARENTS

I say 'roles', not 'role', because (like real parents) they will have to play many. There will, first of all, be times when they have to act as straightforwardly dictatorial authorities: this is something which must not be concealed or disguised from the pupils. When they do this, they should be clearly seen to be doing it: and it is by no means absurd to formalize this in some way, e.g. by wearing a gown or adopting a particular ritual (enter the Housemaster flanked by Prefects: this is a formal House Assembly: the House stands: orders are issued, crisply: 'carry on, sergeant-major': exit the Housemaster. Everyone knows that this means business).

They will have to have a clear set of rules and sanctions (if there were not sanctions, they would not be rules but pious hopes), which must be firmly enforced. By discussion with the prefects and the rest of the house, consultation, house committees, trial and error, and various devices of which I have written earlier,[1] the whole area of rules-and-contracts – a very important area for moral education – can be handled without too much trouble: and, incidentally, handled much more efficiently on a house basis than otherwise. If

[1] Part III.

ultimately necessary, pupils can be transferred to another house or another school. But if the social base is working at all, we should expect only minor difficulties of a disciplinary kind: there should not be the time or the incentive.

This may seem absurdly starry-eyed: are there not 'problem children', thugs, hopeless cases, mentally disturbed adolescents, pupils from irredeemably 'bad' homes, and many others? And will they not give permanent trouble? Well, how much trouble would they give in the army, on a sailing-ship, when playing football, when trying to survive in the jungle? The point is not, or not only, the firmness of military-style authority: there are many points. There is the 'belonging', the expenditure of energy on difficult tasks, the pressure of the peer-group, the 'being wanted', and all the things we have predicated of the ideal family.

The houseparents will have to take extra trouble with the troublesome. This brings us to their second role, which must be frankly stated to be psychotherapeutic: or if the reader is deterred by the clinical or professional image surrounding the word, let us say that their business is to make the pupils more aware of their emotions and more able to cope with them. How much insight and training they can bring to this task would involve us in a discussion of teacher-training, which I cannot enter here. But that is what the task is. They are, after all, not the pupil's 'real' parents: they are mother- and father-figures. They will – inevitably, and it is no use pretending otherwise – attract what some psychologists call a 'transference' situation, in which the pupils will react to them as to their 'real' parents. The houseparents will naturally realize this, and use it *not* to fill the pupils full of their own particular values, nor to probe their personalities for its own sake, but to make them more autonomous: more self-understanding, and more able to face and handle their own feelings – perhaps particularly, in this context, their aggressive feelings.

This role is so important, and so inevitable, that it needs some form of institutionalization. Any housemaster who knows his job at all creates social contexts in which talk flows freely, and rapidly becomes personal and emotional. He invites his pupils to tea, or has them in singly and gives them a few drinks to loosen them up. Without probing or pressure, the talk comes. The pupil is lonely: hates the prefects: feels he is 'no good': is anxious about his success in examinations: doesn't get on with his brother. And so on. After the houseparents have established themselves in the house, it rapidly becomes plain to the pupils that 'emotions' and personal relationships are things that can be talked about, singly or in groups. There will be no harm, and much good, in making regular sessions for this.

Very much more could be written about this role: but I would advise the reader to turn to the professional psychotherapists for advice. What I want to stress here is that we are now at the core of moral education; and that this is something that works (as teachers surely know well enough) by establishing a social base which gives sufficiently wide and frequent opportunity to set up relationships of *trust, informality,* and *emotional closeness.* In such a situation we do not have to put pressure on pupils to become aware of their own feelings: the limitations of pressure are in any case severe. It comes naturally; but the conditions must be there in the first place. Many teachers who have never heard of 'psychotherapy', and to whom the name of Freud is anathema, do a great deal of this already. It is desperately important, and without it half the point of the 'social base' is lost.

Other roles need no lengthy discussion. Sometimes the houseparent will be an equal (in discussion), sometimes an 'academic' authority (when he knows, and is perceived to know, better than the pupils), sometimes a learner, sometimes a guide, and so on. The role, as we have said earlier, follows from the context. To expect houseparents to be ideally flexible in this way is to ask a great deal: but there will be two of them, and they may have the help of other staff-members who are attached to the house in the capacity of 'house tutors', or whatever we want to call them – and this will also allow pupils to form other attachments besides to the houseparents.

Finally, I hope I need not add that one of the houseparents' most important roles or jobs is simply to *be there,* i.e. in the house. Remember the family model: it is the fact that mother (and perhaps father) is *there* that chiefly reassures the child. If it is practical to arrange that the houseparents live on the spot, among their pupils, so much the better: if not, they must have the time to co-exist. Visiting parents are no parents at all.

5. ROLES OF THE PREFECTS

We can be brief here, because many of the points have already been made in other contexts. Prefects (or whatever we want to call them) will act not only as disciplinary authorities, but also as equals, friends, learners, advisers, etc. Unless this tradition is arranged, of course we are liable to what happens at some schools, where 'they don't want to be prefects, because it just means enforcing discipline'. If it is arranged, the roles are obviously rewarding.

Problems naturally arise with senior pupils who are not suitable for all, or any, of the prefect-roles. There are two ways of dealing with this. First, it is possible to create a tradition and an under-standing whereby it is realized, and accepted, that 'being a prefect' is just *one* job (or one set of jobs), for which some are suitable and others not, without loss of face or status. With sufficient interaction and activity on the part of the house, it will become clear that some people are leaders, others advisers, others workers, others researchers and so on: the importance and difference of each will be understood in the course of the activities, and accepted. Secondly, provided that the solid core of older pupils can be made prefects without hesitation, they can 'carry' co-aeval pupils left over; or one can arrange it that they have prefectorial status but special responsibility for whatever roles they *can* perform successfully (e.g. looking after the library). The sensible teacher will solve this problem in terms of whatever system he runs; some, for instance, have 'prefects' and 'prefects' advisers', others have 'senior prefects' and 'junior prefects', and so on.

Whatever the system of nomenclature, there will be a need for one Captain or Head of House, who should be able to run the house as effectively as the houseparents. (It is of course possible to have a dyarchy of one boy and one girl.) There will also be a need to make sure that the prefectorial body is coherent, not at war with itself, and to some degree a special group on its own. This is not to say that they must be allowed or encouraged to isolate themselves: but their role is very important, and they must be able to have somewhere where they can discuss and organize without interference, even if we also distribute them on the topographical system mentioned earlier (one or two in a room of about 20 pupils).

The houseparents will find that, at least where a tradition is already established, they will do well to listen to the advice of the outgoing prefects in making a selection of the incoming ones. It should be a mixture of selection by the houseparents on the one hand, and a kind of 'coopting' system by the prefects on the other. First select, having taken advice from outgoing prefects, your new Captain of House: then pick the others with his help, and with the advice of each one as he is picked. Obviously it is advantageous if at least the new Captain has already been a prefect during the previous year; and of course the more older and abler pupils are willing to

stay on for another year, the better the candidates for selection·
The prefects should be able to keep things running smoothly
without the need for irrational punishments, thereby obviating the
difficulty of how much power to put into their hands. But a tradition
has to be established whereby, if members of the house cause trouble
or oppose the prefects in a way which causes them to bring them to
the houseparent's attention, the houseparent will be expected to
support the prefects – and to be pretty angry (at least) with the
trouble-causing members. Very occasionally the houseparent may
have to overrule the prefects: but he should beware of doing so.

It will be clear that a great deal turns on getting the right prefects:
and the houseparents will think of ways of training. Activities and
institutionalized roles (such as the role of supervising the new
members of the house in certain ways) will provide plenty of
opportunity for training and marking 'cadet' prefects, and the
houseparents should always be thinking in terms of next year's and
the ensuing years' 'material'. The time and trouble spent in this
task will be well repaid by the amount of (educational) work done by
the prefects. Like army NCOs, it should be they who form the
backbone of the house system.

6. AGGRESSION

This is a vague term, and I shall not attempt a philosophical analysis
here. But the reader will recognize it as an adequate title for one of
the most important areas with which the house-system will have to
deal.

It is possible to become slightly clearer by distinguishing the
following:

(a) Just 'letting off steam', e.g. by chopping logs, kicking footballs, etc.
(b) Opposing oneself to others in some (more or less sophisticated)
    competitive way, e.g. in wrestling or chess.
(c) Opposing oneself to a hated or feared group or individual in an
    'institutionalized' form: e.g. if you are a pupil, hate the staff,
    and take part in a football match against them.
(d) As in (c), but not in an institutionalized form (you just swear at
    or punch the staff).

These distinctions are over-simple; if one was doing a proper job
one would have to decide whether to draw them in terms of a
person's *motive* or *emotion* in acting, the *overt action*, or the *type of
consequences intended*. But they will do for a start.

If we knew how far 'aggression-problems' could be solved by methods appropriate to (a), methods appropriate to (b), and so on, we should be in a better position to determine the activities required. Thus most teachers know that, when children are unoccupied (perhaps towards the end of term) or 'fed up', it is then that furniture gets broken and trouble caused. Now, in this or other contexts, do we need (a) simply 'letting-off-steam' contexts (we say 'O.K., run off and chop logs or kick footballs')? Or (b) contexts in which they can compete with each other (tugs-of-war, etc.)? Or (c) contexts in which they can 'get their own back' on staff-members, prefects or other disliked groups (a football match against the staff)? Or (d) will *no* context that *we* (the authorities) provide have any merit, just because it is provided by us – must the aggressive teenager satisfy himself precisely by being aggressive in ways we do *not* want?

I do not think the answer to this question is at all clear; but teachers can try out different possibilities. One important thing is not to be misled by current fashions for 'cooperation' rather than 'competition'. The distinction, made thus simply, is anyway a poor one: for what counts is not the *form* of the activity but the *feeling* which informs it: thus the cooperative activity of building a house together may be, in the most significant sense, 'competitive', if pupils try to gain superiority over each other, look down on poor house-builders, etc.; and conversely the competitive activity of tennis or football may (behind the competitive *form*) amount to something more like a cooperative work of art created by two amicable players. Apart from this, however, it is no use pretending that people do not like to compete, and if possible win: that this is not one way of institutionalizing aggression: and that there is something disreputable about it. Some people (perhaps especially women) will pretend otherwise: but this is usually self-deception. The pupil has to learn to compete, to tolerate both success and failure: for this is not part of 'our wicked competitive system', but a form of life which is inevitable for any society. But he has *also* to learn that there is another, perhaps more important, part of life which is not a matter for competition.

To some extent, indeed (as with some autistic or maladjusted children), the teacher's job may be to *elicit* aggression: this may be some improvement on being totally withdrawn, apparently apathetic, in a semi-permanent anxiety-state, etc. The aggression is there all right, even in the most virtuous-seeming, nicely-brought-up young ladies. It will do its work somehow, whether turned inwards or outwards. Opportunities for expressing it must be provided. The

problem is essentially one of arranging for the appropriate institutionalized forms, which will both elicit and control it.

Of the four categories (a)–(d) mentioned above, I should be
inclined to lay more stress than is usually laid on (c). My guess is that
if enough forms are provided in which the pupils can (in a controlled
context) 'get their own back' on the staff, aggression of type (d)
would be minimal. What can we think of here? Well, having
mentioned staff-matches, we might remember that the one real
advantage youth has over age-and-authority is youthfulness. Teenage boys are more vigorous and athletic than middle-aged house-
masters, teenage girls fresher and prettier than housemistresses. In
skills and knowledge and power and money they cannot compete:
let them then compete in this, and let them glory in it. Let the staff
praise and acknowledge inferiority: let them recognize their (inevitable) feelings of jealousy, admit them, and try to overcome them.
Otherwise the 'conspiracy' theory of education ('it's all a plot to keep
youth down') begins to have a semblance of plausibility.

Another simple-sounding but powerful method is satire. In a
house where the junior members, the prefects, and the staff can put
on short satirical plays about one another, imitating and laughing at
each other's peculiarities and characteristic behaviour, the amount
of undesirable aggression will be considerably lowered. This is a very
old method; and anyway all we are doing is to institutionalize what
pupils, at least, do anyway. But it is well worth employing.

Others will suggest themselves to those teachers who have got the
point: some we have mentioned already (giving pupils the teacher's
role occasionally, getting them to write reports on the staff, and so
on). If the adolescent can fight an institutionalized battle against
his elders, *and* win, *and* still be made to feel that he is loved, accepted
and admired for winning, it may be that we shall find the much-
vaunted 'teenage rebellion' to be not an iron law of psychology but a
result of educational incompetence.

7. SEX AND SEX-DIFFERENCES

I have assumed without argument that the house requires to be
coeducational, not only because research-findings argue in this
direction, but for the more obvious reasons that this resembles the
family model and that any serious moral education would have to
include education in inter-sexual relationships. I shall not argue this
further here.[1]

[1] See my *Logic and Sexual Morality* (Penguin).

Of the various problems which this creates, the problem of actual (physical) sex-relationships seems to me the least. I have dealt with this elsewhere.[1] Here I need only say that the concept of moral education requires that all pupils should have the relevant factual knowledge (GIG), which of course includes facts about contraception: that 'sex-education' is chiefly a matter of developing concern and understanding (PHIL and EMP) in relation to other people: and that it is emphatically *not* a matter of laying down *particular* moral rules about sexual behaviour. As to what public relations may force upon educators in this area, I say nothing: but I would ask the teacher to remember here, almost more than anywhere else, that he is supposed to *educate*. What follows from this he can work out for himself: but he will readily see that the *control* of sexual behaviour is, to say the least, not his main task.

Much more difficult is our choice of activities, and the deployment of the house system in general, in relation to girl-boy differences. The difficulty is caused by our ignorance about the nature and causes of these. There is a vast literature on this, mostly doctrinaire and tendentious. Here we may be content to point to and comment on three views:

(a) Sex-differences (I mean psychological sex-differences, not physical ones) are 'innate': girls are 'naturally' more passive, less aggressive, better at some things and worse at others, and there is nothing we can do about it.

(b) Sex-differences are the result of 'socialization': girls are trained, expected, or brought up to be passive, clean, 'feminine', not to take the initiative, and so on: boys to be brave, active, 'masculine', etc. We can (and most add, should) change this by not 'type-casting' the sexes in this way. Consider societies where the roles are reversed, and where nothing disastrous follows.

(c) Sex-differences are the result of very early childhood experiences, arising from an awareness of significant anatomical differences; this awareness inevitably generates basic mental 'sets', different for girls than for boys. Parents and 'society' cannot do much about it: the girl or boy who denies their basic 'set' goes against her or his own grain.

Respectable evidence on this is hard to collect, because much of it turns on *unconscious* feelings and beliefs, which (for the most part) are available only to clinical psychotherapists. My guess is that (a)

[1] ibid.

is highly improbable, and that the psychological sex-differences we have in most industrialized societies are a mixture of (b) and (c). I should like to stress (c), because I think there is more in it than modern feminists allow (or, unconsciously, want to allow). The teacher will do best if he simply observes what activities boys and girls are *happy* in: what seems to go against the grain, and what seems to go naturally. In any case, most of the 'type-casting' will have been done before the child reaches the secondary age: and it is beyond the teacher's power to restructure the child's whole personality.

Sex will, of course, be one of the topics or areas which the house-parents will discuss in therapy-groups: and the boy-girl interaction will be sufficient for there to be plenty of material, and plenty of opportunity for the relevant emotions to be manifested and considered. These emotions are very strong, and it is no use for the houseparents to try to play them down. However, any well-organized house will be able to avoid constant preoccupation with this area (whether in the form of guilty relationships, 'clinging for security', or any other), simply because there will be too many other things to do. I should guess that sexual interaction would become somewhat more stylized or conventionalized as a result: one would certainly hope for style, though not for 'respectability'.

F. RELATION TO THE ACADEMIC SIDE

In this section we shall not try to indicate what 'academic' or 'class-room' methods of moral education are desirable. I have said something about this elsewhere,[1] and need here only remind the reader of the point made earlier about the nature of the connection between the 'academic' and the 'social' methods.[2] What I want to discuss now is how, in the most general terms, the whole 'academic side' of the school's life fits in with the 'social base' of the house system which we have described.

I. 'SETTING' AND 'STREAMING'

Under this heading we may consider the (regrettably fashionable) problems of how to group pupils academically. The first thing that should strike us is that many of these problems are palliated, if not entirely abolished, by the social base we have set up. For the chief

[1] *I.M.E.*, pp. 411–12.
[2] pp. 98–104.

worry, for many people, about differentiating pupils by strictly academic criteria (I.Q., intellectual attainment, etc.) has been that such differentiation 'type-casts' the pupils socially. The point is, not so much that our criteria for differentiation (e.g., the 11-plus examination) may be unsatisfactory, but that *any* clearly-defined and firmly-used academic criteria will produce fixed groups of 'bright' and 'stupid' pupils, 'failures' and 'successes', children who are strongly expected by all their teachers to perform badly (and who hence often do perform badly), and so on. In the extreme case, 'grammar school' pupils and 'secondary modern school' pupils virtually become two different social classes – or, at least, the segregation reinforces classes that already exist.

But it will now be clear that, if we set up our social base with any degree of success, the pupil's 'social identity' (his feelings of security, confidence, achievement, etc.) will *not* be primarily based on his strictly academic performance. They will be based on his life and activities in the house. That is where he belongs, and where his chief emotional investment lies. This does not mean (as we shall remark later) that his classroom work will be regarded, either by him or his houseparents, as unimportant. But it does mean that his whole identity and status in the school will not be academically governed.

Given this, we may now concentrate on his academic 'grouping' by using strictly academic (not social) criteria. In other words, if for the pure purposes of *efficient learning of subjects* we think it desirable to 'set' or 'stream' pupils by attainment-level, rather than age, or some woolly desire to 'integrate' all the pupils, then we may do so with a clear conscience. We may have, as it seems to me *prima facie* obvious that we ought to have, young pupils who are very advanced for their age in the same class as older pupils: clever sixth-formers in a different room from their contemporaries: and so on. For if the house system works at all, the pupils will appreciate that it is not *these* (or any other particular) variations among human beings which make them 'successes' or 'failures'.

Without a full discussion of this topic, I should nevertheless incline to suppose that academic efficiency would be considerably raised by our new-found ability to set and stream with a clear conscience. For it is a point of logic (not of empirical research) that there are some activities – and these among the most important – which simply *cannot* be undertaken by all pupils. Thus, I cannot do anything that could seriously be called 'discussing *Hamlet*' or 'playing a Beethoven symphony' unless I already have certain attainments and abilities (a knowledge of Shakespeare and competence on the violin). Certain educationally important activities are bound to be 'élitist' activities: not that we should not try to initiate as many pupils into them as possible, but that we have to recognize that people's abilities and attainments differ.

From the moral educator's viewpoint, as well as the academician's, this is important. It would be fatal to put false limits on pupils' abilities; but equally fatal to imply that there are *no* limits. Each pupil has to recognize what he is like, what his academic and other talents are: to rate his own attainments by some standards at particular points in time: to be able to compare these with other people's, and to accept the facts. Any attempt to mask or disguise the true situation is highly misleading for the pupil. Some people *are* more stupid or more clever than others, better or worse at mathematics, French, and other subjects, more or less well-adapted to academic learning. These facts are important: partly because if standards of excellence are to be preserved we must keep them clearly in our own and our pupils' minds, and partly because pupils need a realistic ego-ideal. Both teachers and pupils are perfectly aware of these simple truths.

2. THE FORM-MASTER

Even with the social base of the house, pupils will profit by having *one* member of staff who (if only for a term or a year) is primarily responsible for their academic work. I shall call this the 'form-master', and assume that the pupils' academic day begins at least with him. I should hope that he would be able to cope with most of pupils' basic subjects: amongst these we might, without too much dispute, include language-skills (reading, writing and oral expression), the elements of moral and religious education, and perhaps a grounding in the chief 'forms of thought' (science, mathematics, history). The form-master would be able, with the houseparents' help, to understand the academic abilities and interests of the pupils, and to retain a grasp of their performance even in subjects where he himself is not an expert.

Making sense of the pupils' academic work is largely a matter of becoming clear about the curriculum and the 'forms of thought' just mentioned:[1] and in this light the form-master's role becomes even more important. Between them, the form-master and the houseparents should be able to understand and – more important –

[1] p. 108.

E*

to *motivate* each pupil as much as is humanly possible. With such understanding, we shall be able to demand a great deal of hard work, and shall have much less need to keep the children 'in play'. This makes the organization of the academic side into a much more manageable problem, as we shall now see.

3. MOTIVATION AND MAN-HOURS

Perhaps the 'practical difficulty' that will be uppermost in the minds of many readers is simple *shortage of time*. 'We are up to our ears as it is in the classroom: our classes are too large: we have to prepare them for examinations: how can you expect us to run a house system as well?' The well-informed reader may already have grasped the chief points of an answer to this: but I shall try to spell it out in some detail.

First, we have to get away from the traditional picture of the school as essentially a *custodial* institution, which keeps pupils 'in play' by putting them in classes supervised by teachers from (say) nine to five. Is there, in fact, any reason to suppose that, either from the academic or the social viewpoint, this is an efficient method? Are there not other possibilities, other ways of deploying our teachers and pupils? Isn't it true, in fact, that teachers do *much too much* work in certain respects, with too little results? The following points seem relevant:

(a) Educating is not (only) giving *information*. Information may be given more quickly, accurately and efficiently than by having one teacher facing a class of 30–40 pupils. It may be given by books: by closed-circuit TV: by self-operated cassettes and tape-recorders: by mass lectures. A great deal of teacher-time is spent on giving information; and it is time wasted. The actual amount of *teaching* – that is, explaining, discussing, and any kind of *dialectic* process with pupils – that is required for the groundwork of most subjects, and that has to be done by a single person in a class of 30–40 pupils, is actually very small.

(b) Again given the motivation, we may make wide use of 'free periods', or other systems whereby the pupils pursue their own studies: either unsupervised, or with the opportunity to approach the teacher when they wish.

(c) We may use older or more advanced pupils to teach the younger or less advanced (they often do it better than we do).

All this will free the teacher's time considerably. But, of course, it all depends on adequate motivation: and this, in turn, depends on the social base (and the form-master). The teacher must be used to motivate, to encourage, be stern, make demands, etc. in the *proper setting:* that is, in the *social* setting. The houseparent, having got to know the pupil as a *person*, and arranged for him to have a secure identity in the house, will be able to say in effect 'Right, now then, you're here partly to *learn* something: and we're going to put you in touch with various subject-teachers, who with the help of books and cassettes and TV lectures and so on will teach you all that you need. These subject-teachers will *not* always be worrying about you as a person – that's my job: so it's up to you to profit as much as you can from them. You should find a lot of it quite interesting; but whether you do or not, you'll have to account to me for what you do. If I hear that you're not doing your best, I shall come down on you like a ton of bricks – and so will your seniors in the house: though they'll also help you with your work, and do the best they can for you. But the onus is on you'.

This sounds naïve (though not half so naïve as to suppose that the 'intrinsic interest' of academic subjects will motivate enough): but it can work, *if* the social base is good. And if it is not, no amount of prodding or amusing or anything else by classroom-teachers will do any better. Of course we want good and interesting subject-teachers; of course we need to ensure that the academic content fits the pupil: of course the subject-teachers should not be inhuman robots, but should stimulate the pupils as people also. But this will not be sufficient. We need – not only in order to save teacher-hours, but anyway – so to arrange things that we do *not* have to keep the pupils 'in play' by personal class-supervision for more than a fraction of the nine-to-five 'school day'.

What fraction? This will depend on the school, the pupil-teacher ratio, and many other factors. But to give a quick account, I should estimate that the classroom 'periods' of the average secondary-school should be reduced by *at least 50 per cent*, to be replaced by the methods mentioned above, and freeing the required number of teachers for work within the house system. We incline to cry 'But there just won't be time to teach them enough!' only because we are dominated by the myth mentioned at the start of this section. For the most part, pupils teach and should teach themselves. But the social structure has to be right (remember the family model again). So I do not think that teachers have any real excuse, in terms of man-hours, for not operating the kind of social base we have developed earlier. Not all teachers, of course, will be suitable for all roles: we might wish to distinguish 'subject-orientated' and 'pupil-orientated' teachers, assigning the former to the classroom and the latter to the house system. But to consider the problem entirely in terms of 'reducing the size of classes' is to misconceive it from the start.

4. EXAMINATIONS

I mention this topic chiefly because it is *one* of the 'practical difficulties' that teachers will have in mind on the 'academic' side. I do not want to pretend that it is not a difficulty at all; but much can be done to palliate it, so long as teachers are clear enough and firm enough.

First, I would ask the reader to remember the distinction we drew in Section A between educational and non-educational objectives. Neither 'getting good exam. results' nor pleasing the parents by enabling their children to 'do well in the world' are educational objectives. Teachers may *use* the examination system for educational purposes, but cannot fairly quote it as an inescapable imposition.

I am well aware of the importance of 'public relations', and what the world counts as 'success', for many schools: but teachers need not be their slaves. The teacher knows best how to educate the pupil: what parents and politicians want for (more usually, *from*) pupils must be taken some notice of, but should not be regarded as overriding. Parents and politicians do not own children. Nobody owns them: they are in trust, so that educators can develop them into autonomous adults, doing their best for *them*, not using them to fulfil the partisan desires of others.

A school whose staff is clear about this will be interested in teaching subjects, and will use the examination system only where this does not inhibit or interfere with what it conceives to be good teaching. If a pupil can sensibly take an O Level, or A Level, or whatever nomenclature we are saddled with at any time, without educational loss, well and good. This means either that the school regards the examination as something certain pupils can work *for* : or that the pupil will be able to take the examination *en passant*, in the course of his ordinary education. The latter alternative would, in most cases of examinations as we have them, be in my view the more plausible. But neither case gives the teacher an excuse for saying 'We don't *want* to put pupils in for these examinations, but we *must*'. Teachers must simply be firm with parents, administrators or whoever puts anti-educational pressure on them: they must just say:

'A and B can take exams X and Y without educational loss, in our view: you may want C and D to be taught for these exams, but we're not going to'.

If a substantial number of teachers took this line, we should have no problems in this area: and it is to be hoped that enough will do so to alter the system. Until then, there is of course the difficulty that Johnny requires a couple of O Levels if he is to be a laboratory technician, Molly needs two A Levels to go to university or the college of art, and so on: their friends may achieve these results by being 'crammed', and they will feel 'failures' if they are not crammed likewise and pass the examinations as their friends do. What can the teacher do about this?

Well, he may have to compromise up to a point – *not* because of outside pressure, but in the psychological interests of his pupils, who (like himself) suffer under a grotesque competitive system. Even here, however, he should be careful. Will Johnny and Molly make reasonably *good* laboratory technicians and university students? Is this goal really in their interests, or are they just carried away by fashion or a desire for social betterment ('all my friends go to the university . . .')? This may not be entirely up to the teacher to judge: but a teacher who really knows his pupils will have something to say about it. Indeed, given a good 'social base', my experience is that a trusted teacher should be able to steer Johnny and Molly along the right lines (so far as examinations and careers are concerned) without browbeating or imposition. If Johnny and Molly *really* have these ambitions, they will work hard enough by themselves to pass the examinations: the teacher need not waste man-hours in cramming.

This does not, of course, mean that the teacher will not want to put pressure on the pupils to work hard: nor that he will not want to use *some* examination system. In so far as he does not think the existing one to be educationally satisfactory for his pupils (and in many cases I should agree with him), he may use his own; and, again given the right 'social base', the *school* examinations should be those in which the pupils emotionally invest. At least the pupil must come to understand that it is a tiresome, external system which imposes the public examinations: he had better get them over, if he needs the relevant passes: but so far as *education* is concerned, it is the school which counts.

In using examinations, the teacher must distinguish between the aims of

(a) letting the *pupil* have a clear idea of how he is progressing in a subject:
(b) making sure that the pupil is doing some work and making progress:
(c) giving the pupil a goal to work for:
(d) having a good method of selection for the pupils' future work.

All these are different, and there is no *a priori* reason why the same examination should be used for all four aims. What seems absurd about the existing public system is that their chief function is supposed to be (d): universities and employers need some indication of pupils' abilities and attainments, and O and A Levels (or whatever) are supposed to provide this. In fact they do not provide it effectively: not only do they fail in this, but they also absorb aims (a) – (c), and thereby dictate pupils' work in schools. Given a clear grasp of different aims, it would not be difficult to devise a better system: bearing in mind also the distinctions between being *educated*, being the right sort of person for a particular *institution* of higher education (university, liberal arts college, etc.), and being suitable for a particular *job*. But I cannot pursue this here; I mention it only lest teachers who to some extent replace the public examinations by their own system make the same mistakes as have already been made.

5. CORRELATING THE 'ACADEMIC' WITH THE 'SOCIAL'

All I really need do here is to remind the reader of what was said in Section B. For the purposes of moral education, we have to have a whole range of methods covering the same ground or *content* (either the same moral component' or the same topic).[1] These methods will vary according to how 'practical' or 'real-life' they are on the one hand, and on the other how 'academic' or 'theoretical'. It will be obvious that some of these methods will best be employed in the house system, and others in the classroom.

It is difficult to go into detail here, because which particular methods should be employed where depends very much on how much attention the school is prepared to pay to moral education (and religious education, which is closely connected with it)[2] in general. If for instance the school is unwilling or unable to run anything like a house system, then much will have to be attempted in the classroom which should really be done in the house: conversely, if

---

[1] *I.M.E.*, p. 448 ff.
[2] *E.R.E.*, *passim*.

the school runs a house system but is not prepared to devote any 'academic' time to moral education (even under other subject-titles, such as English or history), then much will need to be done in the house which should be done in the classroom.

But in general it is fairly plain what can most conveniently and effectively go on where; and examples already given in Section B should suffice. In practical terms, this means that we use the house for 'educational experiences' rather than for theoretical study. The pupils engage in some PHIL-type activity (e.g. social service) as a house, and consider this in a more academic way in the classroom periods (e.g. 'social studies'): they have discussion- or therapy-groups (for EMP) in the house, and consider the emotions more objectively in class. And so on. The 'academic' periods for moral education (whatever they are entitled) will be immensely improved if the subject-teacher bases them on whatever the pupils in various houses happen to have been doing immediately beforehand; and in general the task of correlating the two is a large and important one, which teachers will have to work out for themselves.

Much religious education (which I have argued elsewhere[1] to be primarily concerned with the pupil's *emotions*, rather than with his factual knowledge) ought, I would guess, to go on in a house setting; and it is at least arguable that many important abilities, which go beyond the particular aims of moral education, can best be developed there. For instance, the whole business of rational discussion and communication seems to fit the house context: possibly certain skills, arts and crafts could also be based on a situation which is more 'real' than that of the classroom (compare also our remarks on domestic science made earlier).[2] Cooperative project work of all kinds (drama, history, etc.) would also fit here.

Probably more important than any particular suggestions I can make is that the teachers of every school should work out *some* coherent policy. The importance of meshing the academic with the social side is obvious enough: and it is also plain, if I have carried conviction at all, that the social side is not receiving enough attention. If teachers do something about this, they will see for themselves that an overall policy is inescapable: they will have to sit down and work out the necessary details. Naturally they will have to be prepared for much trial and error. I do not pretend that it is easy. But it is essential; and only the teachers themselves can do it.

[1] ibid.
[2] p. 124.

G. Practical Problems and First Steps

This is by far the most difficult section to write, for several reasons. First, schools are in very different positions: some, as I have said, may have been running the essentials of the system suggested for years; others may not even have made the first moves. Some may find no practical difficulties in realizing them: others may be in a very weak position to do so. Secondly, much depends on the administrators: in the case of some schools, they may be persuadable or even eager; in the case of others, they may be ignorant and obstinate. Thirdly, *something* (though not all that much) depends on money: here too schools will be in different circumstances.

More important than all these, however, is the *will* and the *imagination* of the teachers themselves. I emphasize this yet again, because there are so many cases where I have heard teachers say that the practical difficulties are too great. Thus several say 'Oh, yes, that's all right for a *boarding* school: but in a day school like ours, you see, the pupils all go home, and how can you keep them or run a proper house system?' In fact, many day schools *do* run an effective house system: I think, by insisting on some of the features we outlined earlier. Also, the 'day-boy' houses at boarding schools are, or can be, genuine houses. This is not done by magic, or by having 'a good upper-middle-class type of pupil', or a 'charismatic personality' for a headmaster: it is done by taking the need seriously, and working at it.

The fatal move is to accept the existing conventions as given. We do not, for instance, *have* to run our schools on the time-scheme we now employ. We can perfectly well occupy the pupils in some form or other until at least 7 o'clock or even later. We do not *have* to occupy all the teachers all the time, or put all the pupils into classes throughout the day. We do not *have* to use the rooms in the school building as we now use them. We do not *have* to retain the existing dates for school terms and holidays. And so on. Of any suggestion here made, or that the teacher thinks up for himself, the reader should ask 'Is it really impracticable? If we need to persuade somebody, can we really not persuade him? If we need to go through a rather chaotic transition period, or to give more responsibility than we are used to giving to pupils, can we really not risk it? If we need to make time, can we not cut down elsewhere without ruining our pupils' education?'

I hope I have made the point strongly enough. All I can now do is to suggest what some of the first moves might be: these will include what I take to be the essential features among those already suggested. Much of what I say may still seem to be out of reach, or not to apply to this or that school; but I will at least try to be as practical as possible.

1. PROPAGANDA AND PERSUASION

If and when the teachers at the school form a common and agreed policy along the lines suggested, their first task will be to sell it to the relevant people. I take it that this would include parents and administrators: but the first people, on whom all else depends, are the pupils themselves, particularly the prefects and senior pupils. If you can get them on your side, more than half the battle is won. This should not be too difficult. You are, after all, seeking to establish a system whereby they (as much as the staff) are making their own school by making and administering their own houses. Indeed you could do worse than to take their advice (if you are the headmaster) about which members of staff to have as houseparents. It is worth spending a lot of time discussing the system and its details, if necessary changing it at their request: better to set up *any* such system which the senior pupils will back and run (it can always be changed later when they see how it works) than an ideal system which goes against their grain.

Having done this, the teachers (in cooperation now with the pupils) will have a list of what they would like to be done. Some of the items will depend on persuading other people (I nearly wrote 'outsiders': that sounds cliquish, but if you can get the pupils thinking along these lines, it will be a good start). So you need a propaganda campaign, and political pressure. You could start by selling it to the parents, and bringing some of them in to cooperate also; then, if necessary, the education authorities – who, despite my earlier remarks, may well be at least as eager as yourselves to get something done. If you cannot rake up enough money from either parents, or education authorities, or some form of money-making by the pupils, then you have not done the first part of the job well. Make as much of a fuss about it as possible: stress the importance of moral education, social service, 'leadership', 'learning to live' – whatever title will best appeal to those you approach. If absolutely necessary – that is, if you meet with mere obstruction rather than reasoned argument or sheer legal impossibility – then go on strike or make a nuisance of yourselves through the newspapers or in any other effective way.

All this sounds rather dramatic, and it is to be hoped that gentle argument and persuasion will do the job. If made firmly and often and tactfully enough, the chief points are indeed so obvious that it is hard to see how they could be resisted. Once achieve internal coherence – teachers and pupils and anyone else you can win over all seeking the same general objective – and the rest should not be too hard. The exercise will be useful for more than merely attaining its practical ends: it will also help to bind the school together as a social unit, and thereby provide an effective 'social base' from which to take off. It is thus very much to be recommended as a first step.

2. MONEY AND BUILDINGS

Earlier[1] we stressed the need for physical space and *rooms* for each house. It is possible that this problem can be solved by doing without some of the classrooms, or other such devices; but many schools are likely to require more buildings for this purpose. This means more money – unless you can get the pupils, with your help, to construct their own: and even then, you may just not have the space.

First, I should regard the house rooms as having priority financially over much that is spent on other things: for instance, over expensive laboratory equipment. Readjustment of the school's self-controlled budget may be possible. Secondly, it is *not at all* necessary that the 'buildings' should be expensive, or even aesthetically meritorious. (Much money is wasted here.) What is important is that they should be topographically suitable for the house system. I have known houses and house-rooms which, for moral and social purposes, worked extremely well, but which would now be condemned by any respectable local authority.[2] Better that it should be a tent or marquee with oil stoves and candles, than a high-powered modern building which does not suit the purpose.

It is important to establish somewhere, at all costs, which is the 'social space' of the house: anywhere is better than nowhere. Establish this, get the pupils to regard it as their own, and it will be surprising if you and they together cannot expand cheaply enough by some method or other. To make it theirs, it must be as decentralized as possible, not jumbled up with the rest of the school buildings. (I saw one 'house' which consisted of three rooms in a long corridor,

---

[1] p. 112.

[2] Some rooms in the public boarding schools are saved only by their antiquity, I imagine. One of the more tiresome things done by politicians and administrators is to insist on 'modern' conditions (both physical and, allegedly, educational) in defiance of more obvious psychological priorities.

with other non-house rooms in between: of course it failed.) Let the 'binding rituals', and as many integrative activities as possible, go on there: particularly, I would guess, some form of food- or drink-sharing with the houseparents. This is an absolute minimum: you can then add at your pleasure.

3. STARTING OFF A HOUSE

Given some 'house space', what else do we need? The key initial moves, culled from the suggestions made earlier, seem to me to be as follows:

(a) *Houseparents*. Appoint your houseparents first (perhaps after discussion with pupils). So far as possible, relieve them of many other duties: if you can, arrange for them to live in or very near the school. Give them any extra money that is going: more importantly, give them *power*. They must realize that they, and no one else, are responsible for their pupils as people: that, under most circumstances, they will be supported by the headmaster (even, if it comes to that, against the parents and the subject-teachers).

(b) *Prefects*. Let the houseparents, with cooperation from head-master, other teachers, and senior pupils, appoint (say) three or four prefects (to start with) for their house. This needs to be carefully considered, and a lot of time needs to be spent in selection. Bring in the parents if it will help. Having done this, do hardly anything without the prefects. Give them all the responsibility they will carry, and then some more. Reward them as necessary, and give them whatever powers are required.

(c) *House tutors*. With cooperation of all relevant people, appoint one or two house tutors to each house, Ideally these too should live in or nearby, and should have more free time than the ordinary subject-teacher. They must be known to the house, and able to substitute for the houseparents.

(d) *Pupils*. Divide all the pupils in the school *vertically* into as many houses as are convenient. What is 'convenient' here is not chiefly a matter of topography or other considerations, but will depend largely on how many effective 'sets' of houseparents-cum-prefects you can establish. The house should not however exceed 80 members.

(e) *Institutionalizing houses in the school*. Whether or not you have arrived at your houses with the cooperation of the pupils and others, as was suggested earlier in this section (1 above), you need to make it clear that this is how the school is set up. It is not sufficient just to *say* this. You need, for instance, to divide the school up on various occasions (morning assembly, speech-days, concerts, etc.) by houses: to use some social rituals whereby it will be clear that the house system means business. The school can do a lot in this way to give pupils an identity as house-members, even if there are difficulties within the houses themselves; and no opportunity should be neglected.

(f) *Initial experiences.* Here we deal with perhaps the most important feature. As suggested earlier,[1] it will greatly help (particularly if conditions are topographically or otherwise difficult for houses) to bind the house together by some collective experiences *outside* the school – camping, cruising, or anything whereby all the pupils operate as a single unit together with the houseparents. However good the internal conditions for houses, I should be very much inclined not only to start, in each case, by arranging such experiences (even at the cost of 'losing school time' – that ridiculous bogey), but also to repeat them from time to time.

(g) *Making time.* I have not assumed, in (a)–(f) above, that any particular changes *need* have been made in the school's academic structure. But it is plainly desirable that this should have been planned from the first. If it has not been, however, the house system still has great value: and if you have established it so far, now is the time to enlarge and strengthen it, by simply *making time* for house activities. This will involve cutting down class-room periods. Without going into too much detail, I should advocate at least abolishing afternoon lessons, replacing them perhaps with an hour or an hour-and-a-half from (say) 5.30 or 6 to 7 in the evening: in this period pupils may study on their own. This frees the afternoon for house activities. Various schools run various time-schemes of this kind with success, and teachers will have their own ideas. I would only stress, once more, the importance of weaning oneself from the 'custodial' model of the school.[2] Even though there may be practical problems (e.g. about transport to and from school), there is much more scope here than we imagine.

4. TEACHER SELECTION AND MOBILITY

This is important enough to need special mention. You cannot run

---

[1] p. 123.
[2] p. 136.

an effective house system if (a) you have no teachers who want to run one, and are fairly good at it, or (b) such teachers do not stay in the same school for long enough. Plainly much of the problem here can be solved by radically new methods of teacher-training, teacher-selection, and teacher-rewards on a national scale: but something can be done by the school itself.

Make sure, in advertising and interviewing, that you get at least some teachers of the required type. Naturally you need both 'house' teachers and subject-teachers: be clear in your own mind which individuals fall into which category, and that you have enough of the former. Then, so far as you have power, reward them to suit your purposes (presumably after an initial period of probation and inspection on both sides). Above all, make it clear that an appointment as houseparent involves a reasonable length of time: I should regard this as about a *minimum* of four years. 'Special responsibility allowances', or whatever title you use to describe your own money-bestowing powers, should be given partly to *inhibit mobility*.

Much will be gained by putting young members of staff into the position of house tutors: they gain experience, and it becomes clear whether they will make suitable houseparents later. The important thing is to establish something like a *career structure* for the 'social' side of the school, as we now have for the academic side, and as the independent boarding schools already have. 'Being a housemaster' must be seen to be, as in fact it is, a very important job: just as, in a (not much) lesser way, 'being Captain of House'. If these do not flow from the house system as you have set it up, you have set it up wrongly. But you need to make as many moves as possible, when starting the system, to select and reward the teachers who are going to work on this side.

5. COLLECTING EXPERIENCE

As I have said more than once, many of these suggestions are already in force in some schools. The sensible teacher (I hardly need to say) will want to collect experiences from these schools, both before and during his own attempt to implement the suggestions.

It is not necessary that he should actually have worked at such a school; but it is probably necessary that he should have visited one and seen it in action. I have done my best to make the relevant points, but there are innumerable details which the teacher can only collect for himself by actually being there, and perhaps discussing things with the housemaster or (probably better) the pupils. He should not fail to visit schools which are unlike his own in other respects also (social class, boarding, locale, etc.): for many of the points are general, not specific to particular circumstances.

I am constantly amazed at how little the 'independent' and 'state' sectors of our educational system know about each other: and perhaps this accounts for the failure of the latter to cash in on the experience of the former. There is also a good deal of inverted snobbery, and a desire to plough one's own furrow, together with various myths about public boarding schools, which have all helped to confuse the situation. Many state, and day, schools run excellent house systems: but there is much in the boarding schools which would repay attention. This is not to say that there is not much in the state schools which would repay the attention of boarding-school teachers, of course. But state school teachers should not be put off by partisan prejudice (or sheer ignorance).

It would also be extremely useful for *pupils* who are going to help operate the house system to spend some time at a school where such a system works successfully. Much might be gained, on both sides, by having the prefectorial body of a day school spend a few weeks in a boarding school and vice versa. At present schools are incredibly isolated from each other. This needs to be broken down if we are to persuade ourselves, and our pupils, to conduct a serious investigation into moral education and the school community.

6. OPENING UP THE SCHOOLS

Finally, a few general but important remarks about communication. I suspect that one reason why the school community has not been seriously studied, and changed in the required direction, is simply that the *facts are concealed*. Schools tend to be secretive about what actually goes on within their walls, and are naturally suspicious of researchers in this area. More than one researcher has earned the dislike of headmasters who, if they do not resent his actual presence, will certainly resent some elements of his published conclusions.

This is relevant to our concern with practical problems, for so long as those in charge of schools retain this attitude, they will inevitably believe (or act as if they believed) the story which they find it convenient to put out to the public – namely, that 'things are more or less all right as they are', 'there is nothing about the existing school community which calls for radical and immediate change', etc. Suggestions such as I have made in this book become mere abstract theory: something perhaps worth thinking about, but not something which is needed. At the same time those headmasters and other teachers who really want to make changes are inhibited from collecting information from other schools: and hence, by a process of (as it were) mutual denial and retentiveness, nothing gets done.

I do not at all imply that this is wholly, or even chiefly, the fault of teachers. It may be primarily due to the fact that schools are public institutions, are supposed to be 'respectable', are formally or informally supervised by boards of governors, local authorities, parents, and so forth. Hence the teacher who wants to get on with the job (or even to survive) has first to 'square' the outside world: that is, to present and preserve an image of the school such that he is not constantly attacked and interrupted by complaints, doubts cast on his efficiency, 'scandals' in the press, and so on. He cannot afford to say 'Look, this is a rotten school as it stands: the staff are lazy, and some of us are not on speaking terms: the boys and girls do so-and-so and don't do such-and-such: when the pupils leave many of them become delinquent', etc.

Yet this must be true of not a few schools. If the facts are to be known, and if any useful research is to be applied efficiently, it must not be against the will and desires of the teachers themselves: and this means that teachers must be given enough security to be able to open up. Of course it is painful: for some, it may be, in a way, like having to accept criticism of one's own natural children: for others, a threat to one's professional competence. But the good teacher will realize that self-criticism, openness and genuine appeals for help based on the realization of how much needs to be done, are signs of strength. I can do no more here than ask teachers to be brave.

List of Moral Components

It may be useful for the reader (especially in relation to Part I) to have a list of the 'moral components' to hand. Such a list may be more or less simplified: I give here a fairly full version, corresponding to the details of the components in Part I.

PHIL: Concern for people as equals. May be divided into PHIL(1) – justice, respect for other people – and PHIL(2) – benevolence, fraternity, love. Aspects of these are:

    PHIL(HC): having the concept of a 'person' in the required sense: that is, a rational, conscious creature, a source of desires and needs, language-using, etc.

    PHIL(CC): claiming to use this concept as an overriding reason for action: that is, understanding that it is 'being a person' which should generate reasons for action.

    PHIL(RSF): having 'rule-supporting feelings': that is, feelings which support the general rule about acting in others' interests.

EMP: Ability to identify emotions (moods, desires, 'states of mind', etc.)

    EMP (1) (Cs): ability to identify other people's conscious emotions.

    EMP (1) (Ucs): ditto, unconscious emotions.

    EMP (2) (Cs): ability to identify one's own conscious emotions.

    EMP (2) (Ucs): ditto, unconscious emotions.

GIG (1): Knowing facts relevant to moral situations.

    GIG (1) (KF): simply knowing the relevant facts oneself.

    GIG (1) (KS): knowing the 'sources' (where to find out the facts).

GIG (2): Having the relevant 'know-how' or 'social skills'.

    GIG (2) (VC): having this in respect of verbal communication (language).

    GIG (2) (NVC): ditto, in respect of 'non-verbal communication' (facial expressions, gestures, posture, etc.)

KRAT (1): Bringing the above to bear in actual situations:

    KRAT (1) (RA): relevant alertness: noticing moral situations and describing them properly.

    KRAT (1) (TT): thinking thoroughly about them (making full use of PHIL, EMP and GIG).

    KRAT (1) (OPU): ending up by making an overriding, prescriptive, and universalized decision to *act*.

KRAT (2): Translating the decision into action (or feeling).

Bibliography and Sources

The literature is immense, and a great deal of it worthless. What I shall do here is to select a few books which seem to me most immediately relevant to our topics: from these the reader will be able to glean all the further references he needs.[1]

A. *Conceptual theory/philosophy*
This is as important for the practising teacher as for the researcher. A quick introduction are articles by Wilson, Hirst and Peters in *Let's Teach Them Right* (ed. C. Macy: Pemberton Books). On morality and moral education in general, read *Introduction to Moral Education* (John Wilson: Penguin Books), relevant passages of R. S. Peters' *Authority, Responsibility and Education* (Allen & Unwin), R. M. Hare's *Freedom and Reason* (O.U.P.), and *Philosophy and Education* (ed: I. Scheffler: Allyn & Bacon). Clear-headed general accounts of education, with much that is highly relevant to our topics, are *The Logic of Education* (P. H. Hirst and R. S. Peters: Routledge) and – somewhat more advanced – R. S. Peters' *Ethics and Education* (Allen & Unwin). The connections with religious education are explained in John Wilson's *Education in Religion and the Emotions* (Heinemann).

B. *Relevant psychology and sociology*
Undoubtedly the most important work here is that of Prof. L. Kohlberg. The best introduction to this is his article in *Moral Education* (ed. Sizer & Sizer: Harvard), from which further references may be obtained. Derek Wright's *The Psychology of Moral Behaviour* (Penguin Books) is the best general guide. Particularly relevant to Part I of the present book is Norman and Sheila Williams' *The Moral Development of Children* (Macmillan), especially Chapter 6. References to relevant sociology are given in *I.M.E.*, Part II (by Barry Sugarman).

Of equal or perhaps greater importance than all this, in my view, is the teacher's understanding of the psychoanalytic approach: here the best introduction is perhaps J. C. Flugel's *Man, Morals and Society* (Penguin).

C. *Practical Methods*
Excellent accounts of the use of some practical methods are given by

---

[1] See also the Campaign for Moral Education annotated book list (selected by H. J. Blackham): write to National Book League, 7 Albemarle Street, London.

Simon Stuart (*Say :* Nelson) and A. J. Grainger (*The Bullring :* Pergamon Press), amongst others. Books for older pupils include John Wilson's *Moral Thinking* (Heinemann) and *Ideals* (Lutterworth Press): the works of Alan Harris (e.g. *Questions about Living :* Hutchinson) may also be recommended.

Some sources for pupil-teacher material are as follows:
Schools Council Moral Education Project : write to Peter McPhail, c/o Dept. of Educational Studies, 15 Norham Gardens, Oxford.
Farmington : write to John Wilson, 4 Park Town, Oxford.
O.I.S.E., write to O.I.S.E., Bloor Street, Toronto, Canada.

The best (in a sense the only) journal is the *Journal of Moral Education*, published by Pemberton Books, 88 High Street, Islington, London.

Index

Most topics are covered under their own chapter-headings, which are given on the Contents page; but the reader may find the following brief references of some use.